WILLIAM BLAKE

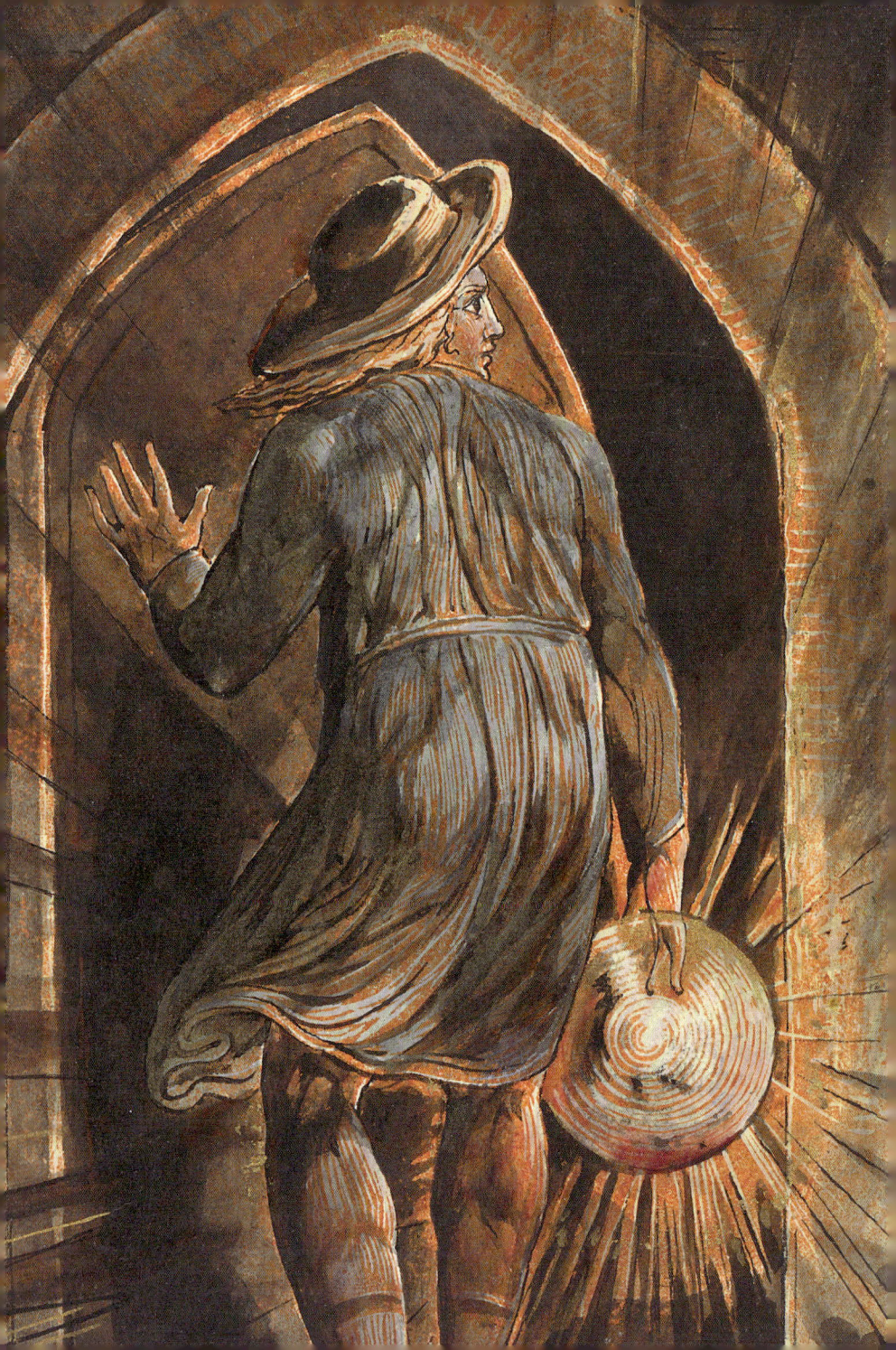

WILLIAM BLAKE

CAROLINE ANJALI RITCHIE

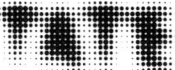

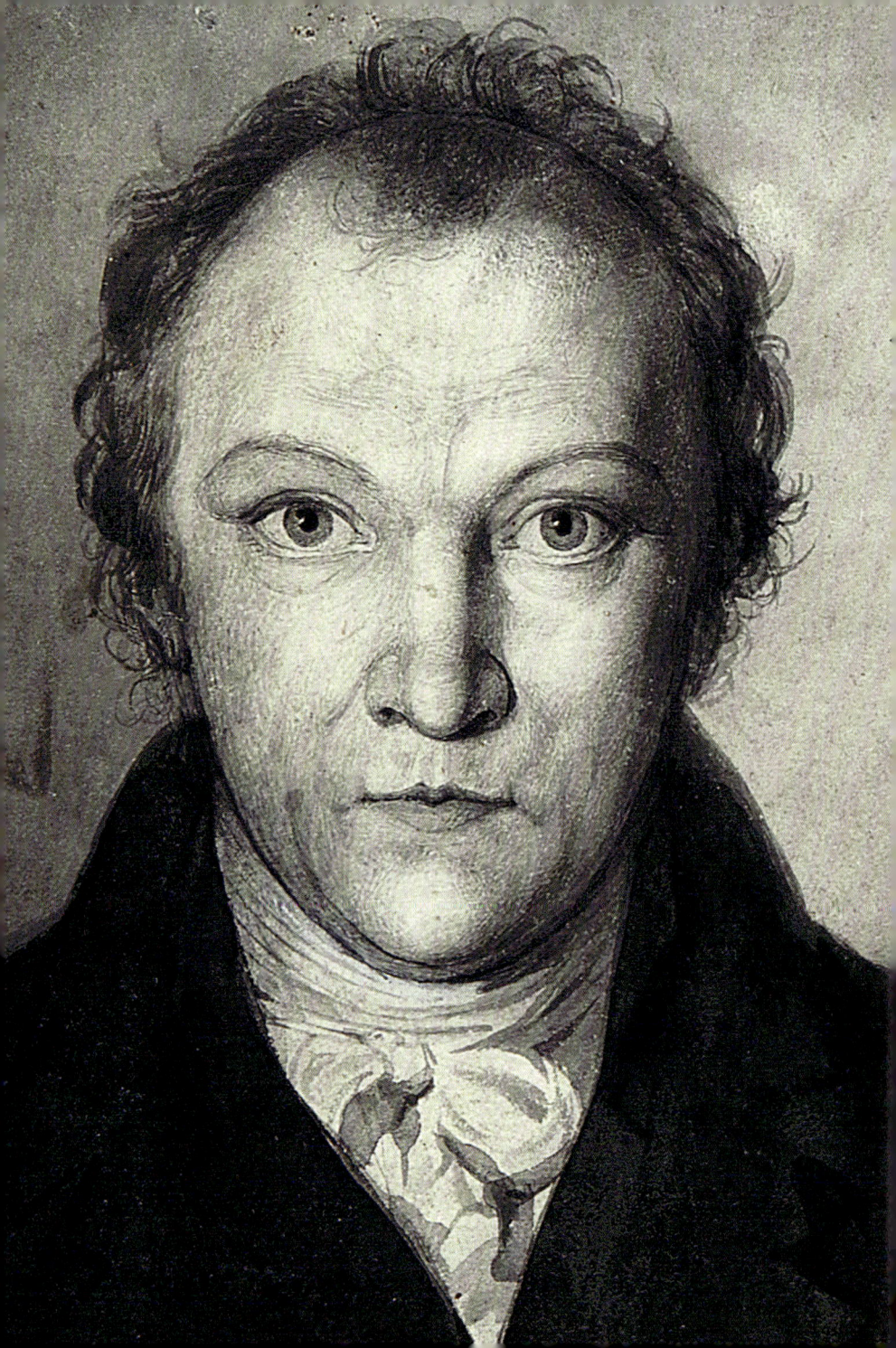

Exuberance is beauty – William Blake.[1]

The artist and poet William Blake (1757–1827) is renowned today for his exuberant imagination and distinctive style. But Blake was not widely appreciated in his own day, and was even considered 'mad' by some contemporaries because of his eccentric personality and ideas. More recently, he has been celebrated as a free-thinking radical, a visionary and a champion of creative freedom. One possible reason that Blake is so loved today is that he fought for artistic success against the odds, challenging established ways of thinking and creating. Indeed, Blake is now often considered to have been *ahead* of his time, appealing to modern ideas about liberty, social justice and artistic experimentation. His recent cultural impact extends from 1960s counterculture to horror films, video games, pop music, protest posters and beyond. This book is a beginner's guide to the world of William Blake, tracing his career through a series of extraordinary artworks.

POET & ARTIST

Painting, as well as poetry and music, exists and exults in immortal thoughts.[2]

Poetry and pictures were equally important to Blake's creative vision, but his primary livelihood was as a visual artist, chiefly an engraver. He cut his teeth as an engraver's apprentice in the 1770s and later took on numerous commissions for prints and paintings. Blake approached these projects with great imaginative energy, but often bemoaned his financial dependence on what he called 'the meer [sic] drudgery of business'.[3]

Aside from these commissioned artworks, Blake was devoted to making self-published poetry and picture books that he called his 'illuminated' or 'prophetic' books. He used an experimental copperplate printing technique devised to integrate words and pictures. Blake's wife Catherine (née Boucher) helped him considerably with printing and hand-colouring these works, which laid out his philosophical ideas through an increasingly elaborate personal mythology. Although an early biographer described the books as 'dark mazes',[4] Blake's work is not entirely obscure or removed from the realities of his time. His poems, prints and paintings directly address major historical events, including industrialisation, revolution and the transatlantic slave trade.

Attributed to William Blake
Portrait of William Blake
1802–4 (detail)
Graphite with black, white and grey washes on paper
24.3 × 20.1

EARLY LIFE

Thank God I never was sent to school
To be Flogd into following the Style of a Fool.[5]

William Blake lived most of his life in London. He was born on 28 November 1757 at 28 Broad Street (now Broadwick Street) in Soho. On this site Blake's family ran a hosiery shop, later taken over by his brother James. Blake's artistic leanings were recognised early, and at the age of ten he was sent to Henry Pars's drawing school on the north side of the Strand.

The decision to send Blake to drawing school rather than for regular schooling may partly have been prompted by the boy's wayward imagination. From an early age, Blake claimed he saw visions of gods, angels and devils; at the age of eight, he apparently saw an angel 'bespangling' a tree on Peckham Rye, South London.[6] Such vivid visions occurred throughout his life, providing inspiration for his powerful artistic imagination. But Blake's artistry was also rooted in technical training. As he later wrote, 'No one can ever Design till he has learnd the Language of Art by making many Finishd Copies both of Nature & art.'[7] At Pars's drawing school, Blake would have learned basic draughtsmanship by copying from plaster casts of classical sculptures.

APPRENTICESHIP

I devoted myself to Engraving in my Earliest Youth.[8]

The launching point of Blake's career was his apprenticeship, aged fourteen, to engraver James Basire of Great Queen Street, Holborn. Basire, who belonged to an established family of engravers, had been appointed engraver to the Society of Antiquaries in 1755 and specialised in architectural subjects. Many of his engravings depicted British buildings and historical subjects and were published in antiquarian books and journals. Although his linear style was becoming increasingly unfashionable with the rise of more painterly rendering, this linearity had a lasting impact on Blake's work: years later, he described his commitment to 'firm and determinate lineaments' in his prints and paintings.[9] Apprenticed to Basire from 4 August 1772 for a period of seven years – the standard duration of apprenticeships at this time – the young Blake was enlisted in a Basire-workshop project to prepare engravings for two different texts describing the monuments of Westminster Abbey. The abbey later became a key landmark in Blake's mythological work, embodying the

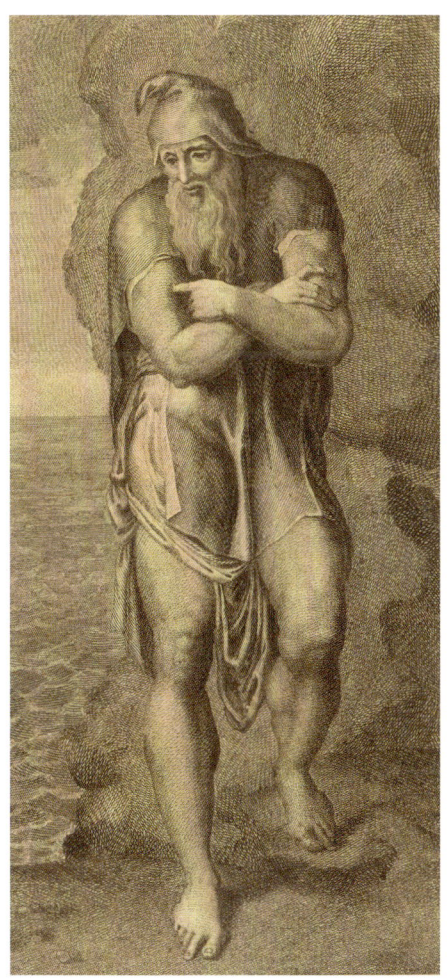

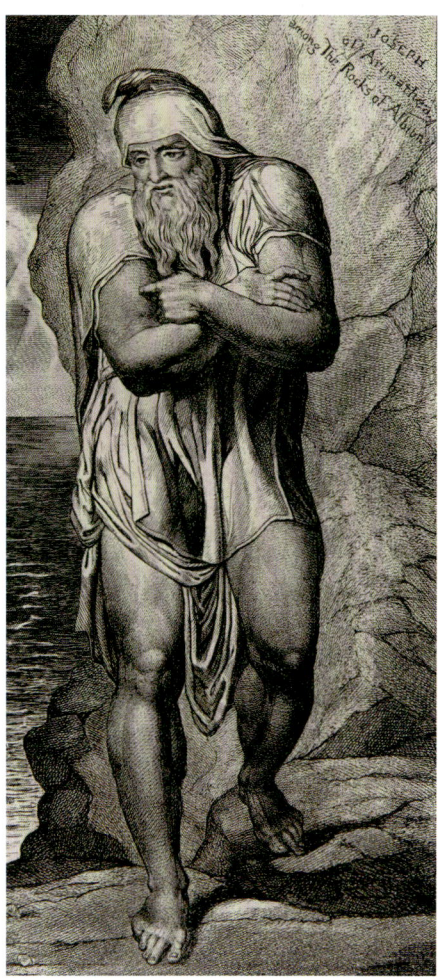

Untitled c.1773
Etching and engraving
on paper
22.9 × 11.9

Joseph of Arimathea Among
the Rocks of Albion c.1820–5
Etching and engraving
on paper
22.9 × 11.9

spirit of gothic art, which Blake preferred to the classical form exemplified by St Paul's Cathedral.

The projects that Blake worked on during his apprenticeship shaped his pictorial style and awakened a lifelong interest in the antiquarian history and legends which pervade his illuminated books. The first standalone plate he is known to have engraved – a print thought to have been produced in 1773, during the early years of Blake's apprenticeship – depicts a cloaked man walking along a rocky shore (above). Here we can see the young Blake practising the technique of crosshatching to differentiate between light and dark. Much later (c.1820–5), he returned to

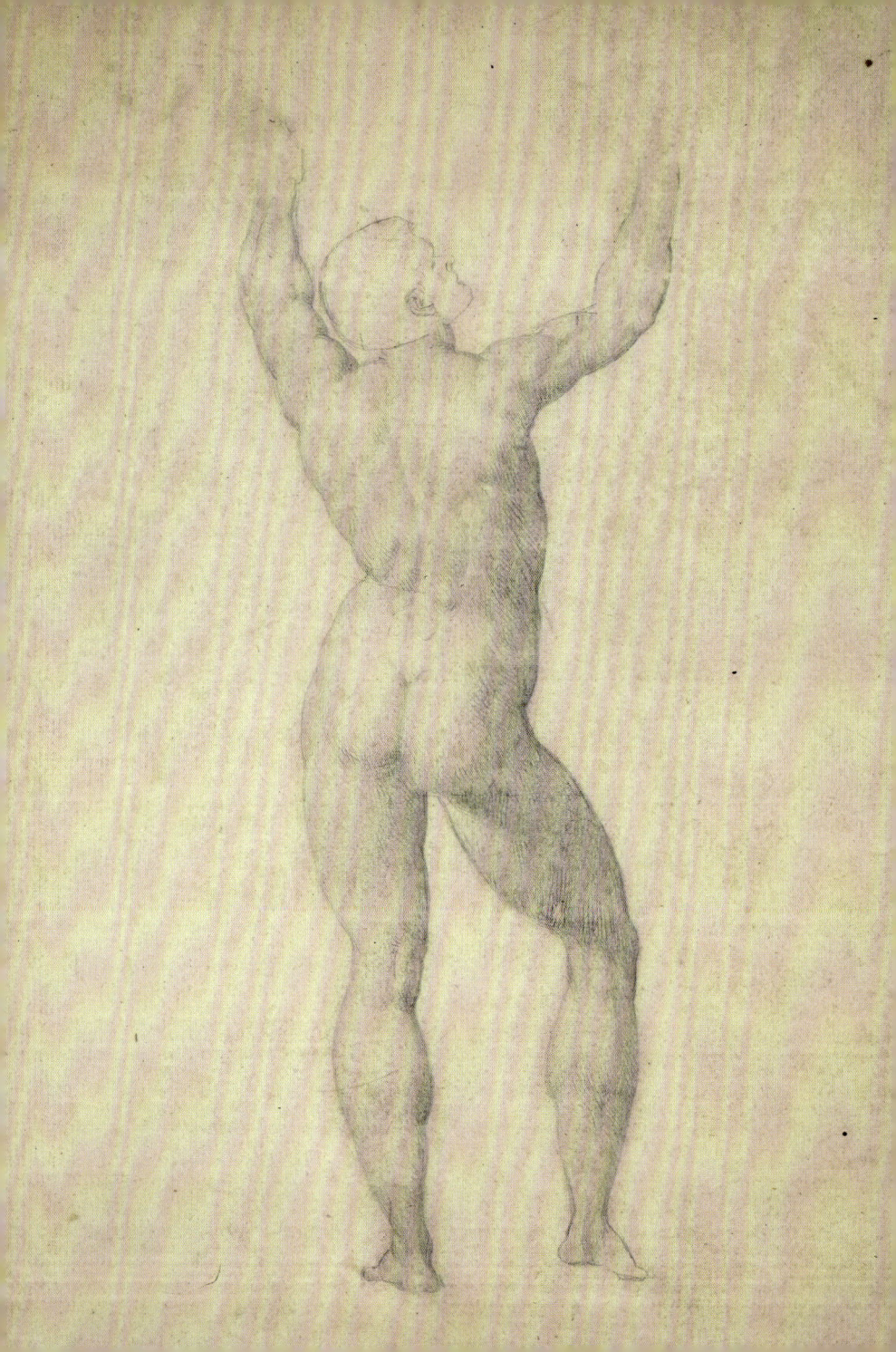

this composition, producing a much bolder, more confident rendering to which he added an inscription stating that the print was originally '[e]ngraved by w. Blake 1773 from an old Italian Drawing' (p.7). The drawing Blake saw was itself based on a figure from Michelangelo's *The Crucifixion of Saint Peter* in the Vatican. Blake also added a title to the later version identifying the subject as 'Joseph of Arimathea among the Rocks of Albion', a reference to the legend that Joseph had visited Glastonbury, bringing Christianity to England.

THE ROYAL ACADEMY

In 1779, Blake's name was entered into the register of students at the Royal Academy (founded in 1768), although it is unclear how regularly Blake attended the academy.[10] Based on some surviving sketches, it seems that when he did attend, Blake studied and drew models from life, then a standard part of artistic training (opposite). The anatomically detailed nude figures appearing in Blake's later work perhaps speak to the impact of this training on his artistic imagination and technique.

Blake did not work in large-scale oil painting, which was the kind of art commonly displayed at the Royal Academy's annual summer exhibitions. He did, however, make some early forays into large-scale history painting, producing three watercolours depicting scenes from the biblical story of Joseph, which were exhibited at the Academy in 1785. He also made pictures based on scenes from works by Shakespeare, which were popular subjects for artworks at the time, such as *Oberon, Titania and Puck with Fairies Dancing* c.1785 (pp.28–9).

Blake later became disgruntled with the Royal Academy. He particularly despised the fashionable style of oil painting advocated by its first president, Joshua Reynolds, whom Blake disliked personally, later writing that he had 'spent the Vigour of my Youth & Genius under the Opression of St Joshua & his Gang of Cunning Hired Knaves'.[11] Nevertheless, while at the academy Blake had a valuable opportunity to meet other artists, such as Thomas Stothard and John Flaxman, and he went on to collaborate with both these artists, producing, for instance, a title-page vignette based on a design by Stothard for John Bonnycastle's mathematical textbook *An Introduction to Mensuration* (1782) (pp.26–7). This work is one possible precursor to Blake's famous print *Newton*, discussed later in this book.

Academy Study: Standing Male Nude Seen from Behind
c.1779–80
Graphite on paper
35 × 22.6

COMMERCIAL ENGRAVING

Blake's engraving of this vignette after Stothard's design was commissioned by the London bookseller and publisher Joseph Johnson, who was based at 72 St Paul's Churchyard. Johnson's shop, and particularly the dining room in his upstairs home, was a hub for intellectual discussion between now renowned dissenters, radicals, artists and educationists, among them William Godwin, Mary Wollstonecraft and the Swiss-born artist Henry Fuseli. Blake began producing plates for Johnson's books in 1782, and the publisher was Blake's most regular employer during the 1780s and 1790s.

Blake briefly set up a print publishing business with his fellow Royal Academy student James Parker from 1784–5, but the business did not take off. Instead, Blake was obliged to accept commissions for reproductive engraving from other

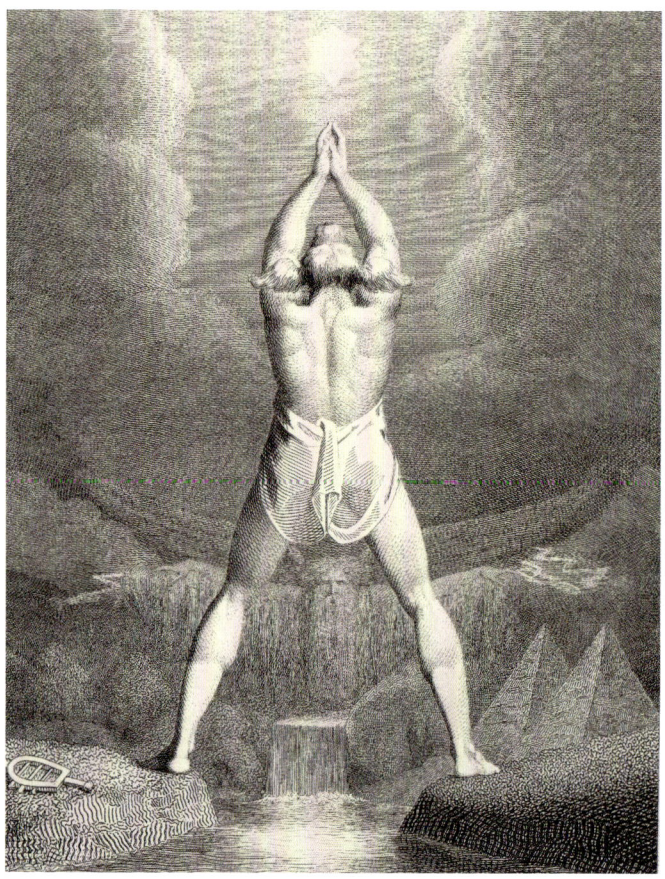

The Fertilization of Egypt 1791
Etching on paper
19.3 × 15.3

The Great Red Dragon and the Woman Clothed with the Sun
c.1803–5
Ink and watercolour over traces of graphite and incised lines on paper
55.1 × 43.3

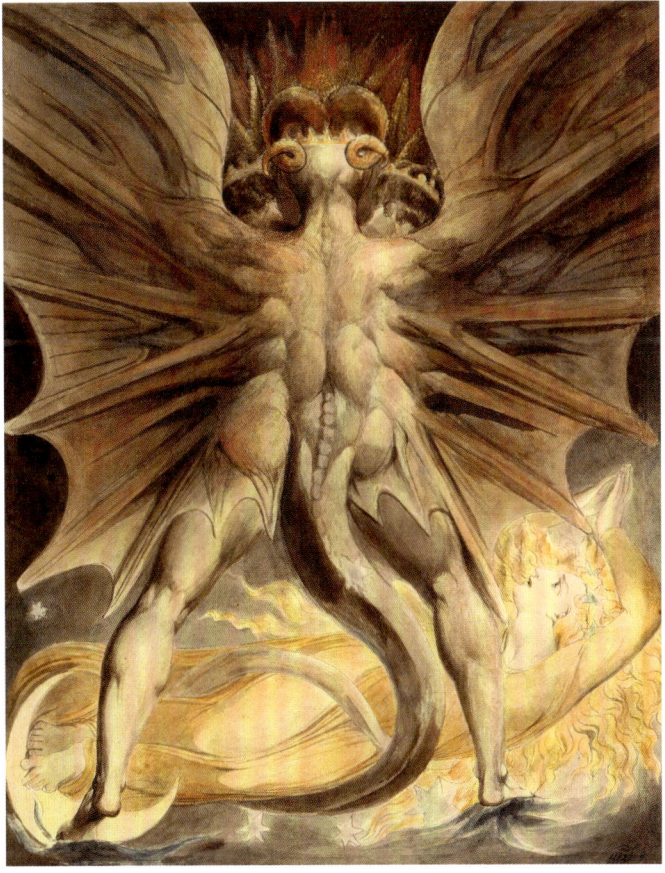

quarters. He engraved a great many plates for Johnson's books, including Mary Wollstonecraft's educational text *Original Stories from Real Life* (1791, 1796) and Erasmus Darwin's book of poems *The Botanic Garden* (1795). Among the plates Blake made for the latter was an engraving after a design by Fuseli: entitled *The Fertilization of Egypt* (opposite), it depicts the Egyptian god Anubis, a dog-headed figure, praying to the star Sirius for rain. Blake echoed this composition in his later watercolour *The Great Red Dragon and the Woman Clothed with the Sun* c.1803–5 (above) (the work features prominently in Brett Ratner's 2002 film *Red Dragon*, part of the Hannibal Lecter film series). His recourse to Fuseli's design in this later artwork registers the close affinities between Blake's mythological paintings and Fuseli's uncanny, monstrous imagination.

Another noteworthy engraving project from this time was Blake's series of seventeen prints for a 1796 book by John Gabriel Stedman entitled *Narrative, of a Five Years' Expedition, Against the Revolted Negroes of Surinam*. Blake's engravings appeared alongside contributions from other artists including Francesco Bartolozzi, Thomas Conder and Inigo Barlow. This text was written at a time of mounting pressure within Britain to abolish the transatlantic slave trade, but Stedman did not have this cause in mind: a Dutch-born Scottish soldier, he had served in Surinam on the north coast of South America as part of a Scots brigade formed to suppress the rebellion of enslaved African plantation workers. His *Narrative* advocates the reform of the slave trade, but not its abolition.

Blake's plates for Stedman's *Narrative* are very vivid, often depicting acts of extreme violence. These highly detailed works clearly indicate a great deal of labour and dedication on Blake's part. What is less clear is how the pictures can be understood in relation to the realities of the slave trade or the abolitionist cause in Britain. It has been pointed out that Blake tends to Europeanise the people of colour represented in these works: this can be seen in his plate *Europe Supported by Africa and America* (p.38), which imposes on its subjects an idealised European body type based on the tradition of the 'three graces' as commonly depicted in European art. In 2015, artist Sokari Douglas Camp reimagined this artwork in the form of a sculpture, which bears the same title as Blake's print but seeks to harmonise the three women, clothing them in Nigerian fashions. More broadly, the Stedman engravings have had an enduring legacy in literary and artistic depictions of the violence of slavery. For instance, some of Blake's and Bartolozzi's plates for Stedman's *Narrative* were reproduced in David Dabydeen's *Slave Song* (1984), a series of poems written in Creole from the imagined perspectives of enslaved people of African descent and Indian indentured labourers in Guyana.

At the same time that he was working on the Stedman plates, Blake produced his illuminated book *Visions of the Daughters of Albion* (first printed 1793) (pp.35–7). Some scholars have interpreted the critical attitude towards enslavement expressed in this illuminated book as supporting abolition; others argue that Blake is here using slavery as a metaphor for the oppressed state of women in Britain, rather than mounting a sustained critique of the transatlantic slave trade itself.

Blake later complained of his 'dependence' on engraving commissions, but such work remained a vital source of income throughout his life.[12] In any case, around the late 1780s, Blake was evidently quite established in his profession, for he took on an apprentice named Thomas Owens. It is unclear how long Owens remained with Blake, although his tenure seems to have been relatively short. Blake's association with Joseph Johnson dwindled towards the end of the 1790s, partly because Johnson was imprisoned for six months in 1799 for publishing a tract that was deemed seditious, after which his publishing activities significantly declined.

CATHERINE BLAKE

1782, the year of Blake's earliest-known work for Johnson, was also the year of another important union – the marriage of William Blake to Catherine Boucher on 17 August at St Mary's Church in Battersea. Catherine's role in William's life, career and legacy has not tended to be fully acknowledged. In fact, the labour she performed was pivotal: she helped with printing and colouring the illuminated books, and provided William with essential care and support.

Catherine Blake was also an artist in her own right. One

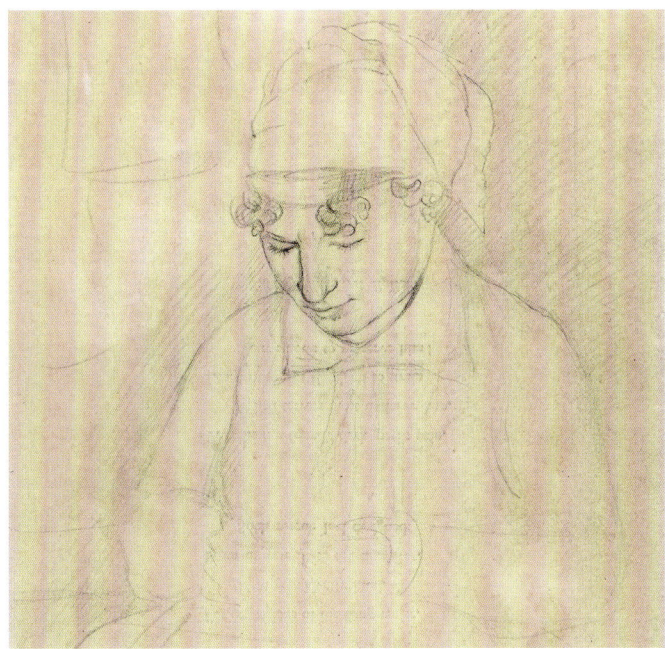

Catherine Blake c.1805
Graphite on paper
28.6 × 22.1

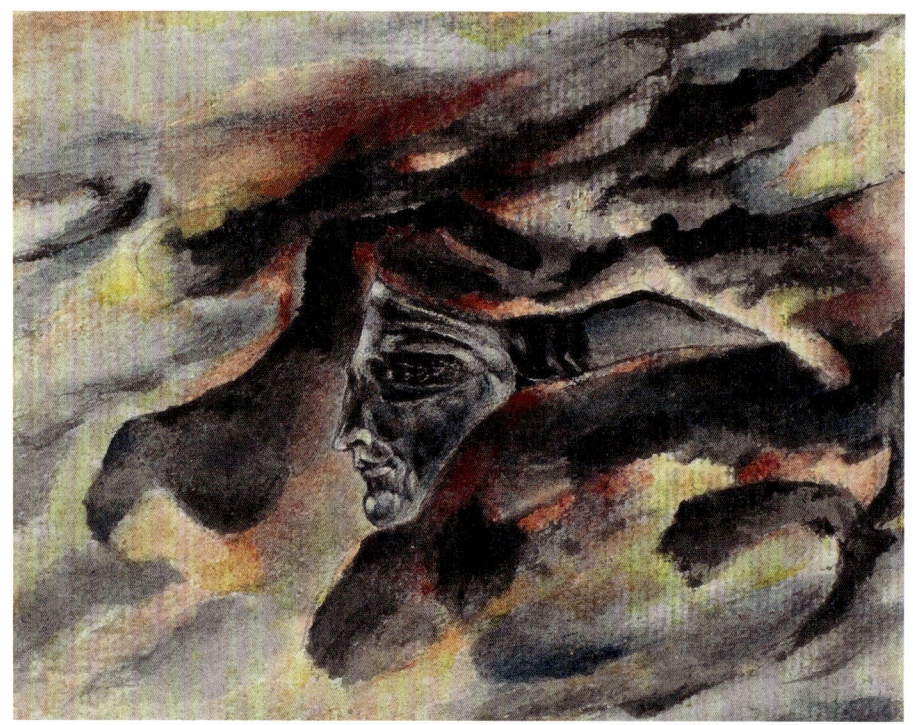

of only two surviving paintings attributed solely to Catherine's hand is the drawing *Head 'taken from something she saw in the fire'* c.1830 (above), its title based on Catherine's description of the artwork as recorded by its first owner, Frederick Tatham. Strange and visionary, the picture recalls William's own accounts of seeing 'visions' and attests to Catherine's sense of the expressive effects of colour, to which she would have become attuned while helping to hand-colour copies of the illuminated books.

Catherine's role as salesperson and custodian of William's art following his death went a long way in ensuring the survival both of the works and of her husband's name; indeed, Blake's biographer Alexander Gilchrist called Catherine an 'excellent saleswoman'.[13] After her husband's death, Catherine also printed new copies of the illuminated books using the original copperplates, and her efforts significantly contributed to Blake's posthumous recognition.[14] Catherine Blake was recently the subject of Sasha Dugdale's Forward-prize-winning poem 'Joy' (2016).

Catherine Blake
Head 'taken from something she saw in the fire' c.1830
Watercolour on paper
9.7 × 12

Tyger Tyger, burning bright,
In the forests of the night;
What immortal hand or eye,
Could frame thy fearful symmetry?[15]

Alongside his artistic training, Blake cultivated an interest in poetic composition. He wrote several short poems between 1769 and 1777, compiled in the volume *Poetical Sketches* (1777). In the mid-1780s, Blake contemplated bringing together his poetry and visual art, composing a manuscript mythological poem, *Tiriel*, for which he also produced a series of twelve wash drawings (nine of which survive). In its sprawling scope, mingling of mythological traditions and accompanying pictorial designs, *Tiriel* was an early precursor to the illuminated books Blake began devising later in the 1780s.

His earliest-known attempts to integrate text and image using his relief etching technique were two small books comprising prose aphorisms and simple visual designs, entitled *All Religions are One* and *There is No Natural Religion* (both engraved in 1788, although the former was not printed until 1795). His first book of integrated poetry and art was *Songs of Innocence* (1789) (p.31), supplemented in 1794 by the companion piece *Songs of Experience*. In the same year, the two volumes were merged as *Songs of Innocence and of Experience* (p.17).

These two books are probably Blake's most accessible works in illuminated printing. The poems use a deceptively simple, sing-song rhythm, while the visual designs are attractive and quite detailed – especially considering the minute scale on which Blake was working – but also rather simple relative to the engravings he produced for other books in the 1780s and 1790s. While the childlike quality they evoke has often led to comparisons with children's books, the apparent simplicity of the language and pictures belies complex and often very dark themes. We enter gloomy territory in the darkly sublime musings of 'The Tyger' (p.32) and in the depictions of urban poverty and malaise in 'The Chimney Sweeper' and 'London' (p.34). These poems reflect Blake's split attitudes to the capital: he was acutely aware of the miseries of city life, and in 'London' famously wrote of the 'mind-forg'd manacles' governing the urban populace. But he later described the capital as a 'wonder of God' and was hopeful about the possibility of creating better conditions for its inhabitants.[16]

The combination of rhythmic lucidity and psychological depth in *Songs of Innocence and of Experience* has inspired many composers to set the poems to music, including Ralph Vaughan Williams, Benjamin Britten and Jah Wobble. American beat poet Allen Ginsberg was particularly inspired by Blake's poem 'Ah! Sunflower' and made recordings of his musical renditions of the *Songs*, released in 1970.

Blake's personal mythology also began to emerge around the 1780s and 1790s. There were early indications of his capacity to dream up imaginary lands and characters in *The Book of Thel* (c.1789).

By autumn 1790, Blake and Catherine were living at 13 Hercules Buildings in Lambeth, South London. The Lambeth years proved extremely productive for Blake, seeing the printing of several editions of *The Marriage of Heaven and Hell* (1790), *Visions of the Daughters of Albion* (first printed in 1793), the three books often referred to as the 'Continental Prophecies' – *America: A Prophecy* (1793), *Europe: A Prophecy* (1794) and *The Song of Los* (1795) (pp.38–41) – and further mythological works entitled *The First Book of Urizen* (1794), *The Book of Los* (1795) and *The Book of Ahania* (1795).

These books took on highly original, often arcane subject matter, but they also relate to historical events from Blake's day. *America*, *Europe* and *The Song of Los* examined both the American Revolution of 1783, which had established independence for Britain's thirteen colonies in America, and the French Revolution of 1789, an effort to overthrow the aristocratic old order in France and establish the rights of the populace (pp.39–42). Blake's poetry calls for emancipation, in a spirit by turns hopeful and forcefully apocalyptic. Similarly, the visual designs to these prophetic books often depict cataclysm: several images in *The First Book of Urizen* show naked human forms chained or interlaced with flames, bodies imprisoned and tortured (pp.43–6). This apocalyptic theme, evoking the trauma and bloodshed of war and revolution, was common in late-eighteenth-century prints and paintings. The mythological figure of Urizen, who is associated with uncompromising rationalism, appears as the antagonist in the video game *Devil May Cry 5* (2019), developed by Japanese company Capcom.

In 1793, Blake printed a 'Prospectus' advertising his books for sale. He claimed that his method of integrating poetry and pictures made the books cheaper to produce than their

Title page to 'Songs of Innocence and of Experience' (Copy C) 1794
Relief etching with colour printing and hand-colouring on paper
Plates range between 12.4 × 7.9 and 10.9 × 6.3

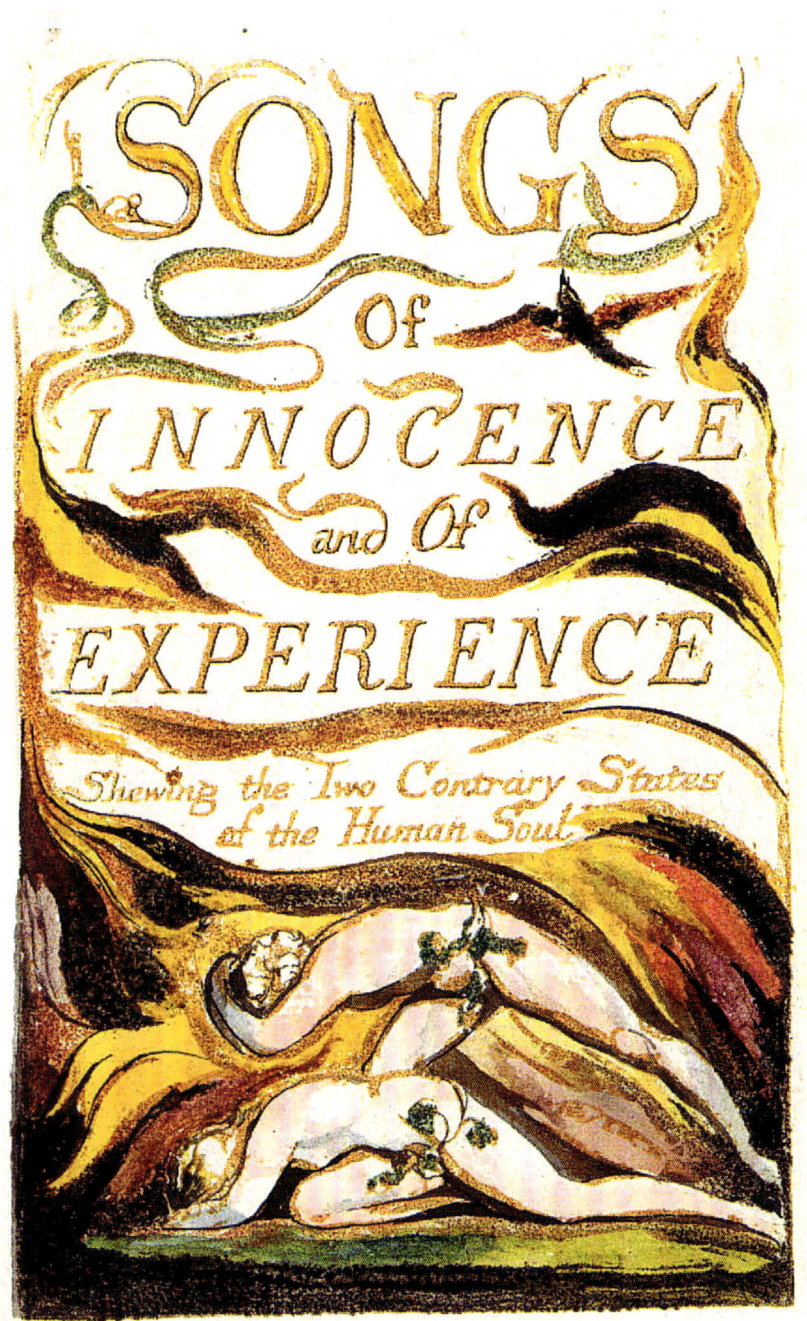

letterpress counterparts. Presumably, then, he had some hopes of turning a profit, but in reality, the Blakes never made much money from the illuminated books. Blake was always obliged to accept commissions for other projects to make a living – but this did not stop him from approaching such projects with the full force of his extraordinary imagination and capacity for technical innovation.

During the Lambeth years, Blake had begun to receive commissions for exciting projects, including a set of illustrations for Thomas Gray's *Poems* commissioned by John Flaxman and his wife. But there were disappointments, too: in 1797, he was invited to make a series of designs for an illustrated edition of Edward Young's poem *Night Thoughts* (1742–6) for the publisher Richard Edwards. Blake proceeded to create 537 highly imaginative preparatory watercolour designs, as well as producing forty-three engravings for the first of the poem's intended four volumes (pp.56–7). However, Edwards left the publishing business around 1798, and the remaining volumes never materialised.

FELPHAM

In an 1800 letter, Blake declared: 'I call myself now Independent… I can be a Poet Painter & Musician as the Inspiration comes.'[17] His newfound sense of 'independence' no doubt sprang from the immensely productive period he had enjoyed in Lambeth and the interest he was receiving from new patrons, among them the poet William Hayley. In 1800, Hayley invited William and Catherine to live in a cottage that he owned, near his residence in Felpham on the Sussex coast. The Blakes' acceptance of the invitation may partly have related to Catherine's poor health at the time, but Blake also relished the coastal setting and was grateful to Hayley for the opportunity. In November 1800 he signed off a letter to Hayley referring to himself as the 'Enthusiastic, hope-fostered visionary, William Blake'.[18] The Blakes remained at Felpham until 1803, by which point Blake's optimism had waned considerably.

During the Felpham years, Blake undertook, increasingly begrudgingly, several commissions for Hayley, including a series of portraits and plates for Hayley's poetry books. This work did not excite Blake: his correspondence from the time reveals his growing resentment towards Hayley and a feeling that his talents were going to waste. In a letter dated January

1803, he complains of his 'dependence' on 'Engravings I have in hand for Mr H'.[19] The artistic disappointments of this period were compounded by another distressing event, in which Blake was accused of uttering seditious words criticising the King. The charges cast a long shadow over the Felpham years, and although Blake was eventually found innocent, his 1804 trial was an extremely traumatic event: if found guilty, he would likely have faced imprisonment or transportation to the colonies.[20]

Despite these tribulations, Blake emerged from this period resolute in his artistic ambitions. By April, he wrote of his delight to be returning to London to 'carry on my visionary studies in London unnanoyd'.[21] Soon after, he described his work on 'a Sublime Allegory which is now perfectly completed into a Grand Poem':[22] this is usually understood to be the long poem *Milton*, one of Blake's major illuminated books of the early nineteenth century (discussed in more detail later in this book). A small vignette Blake included in *Milton* showing himself walking in the garden of Hayley's cottage at Felpham (p.23), where he claimed to have seen a vision, suggests that he did derive some inspiration from his time at Sussex, despite its unceremonious conclusion.

PATRONAGE BY THOMAS BUTTS

The disappointments of Felpham did much to dim Blake's spirits. In general, he greatly lamented having to rely on external commissions from patrons whose demands he resented. While none of Blake's relationships with his patrons was without its complications, nor were all these interactions entirely disappointing or artistically constraining. For example, Blake seems to have had relatively positive interactions with Thomas Butts, who would prove to be one of his most consistent patrons during the early nineteenth century.

Blake became acquainted with Butts during the 1790s. Butts was a civil servant whose primary duties were in military administration, keeping records of enlistments, deaths and the supply of equipment to the army – an occupation that gave him a robust salary to finance his art patronage. It is unknown how the two men met, though they may have been introduced by a mutual acquaintance such as John Flaxman. Butts took a great interest in Blake's work: he and his wife accumulated up to 200 of Blake's artworks, including copies of illuminated books and several additional prints and paintings that they

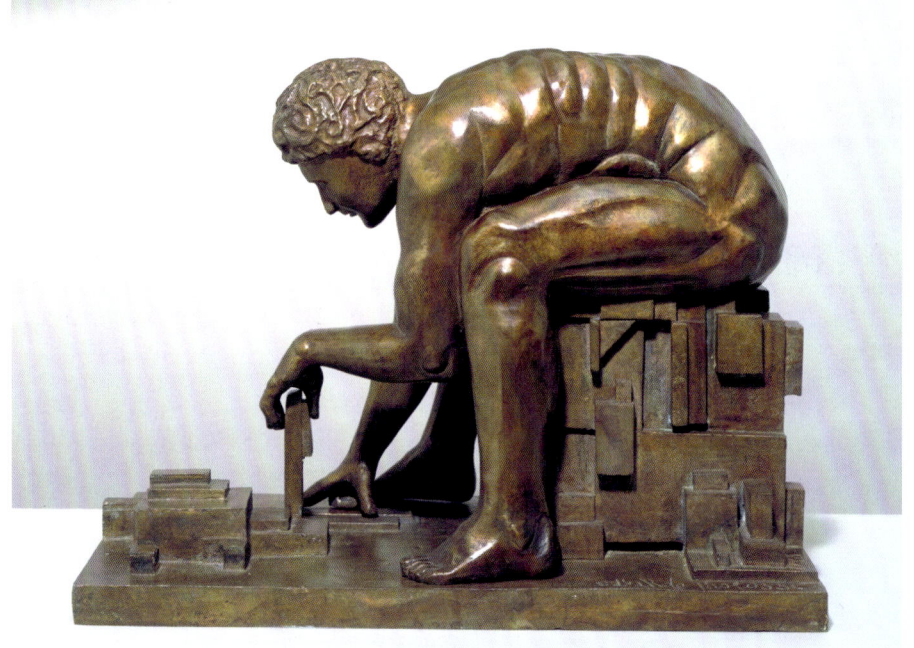

Eduardo Paolozzi
Newton 1988
Bronze
44 × 33 × 60

had directly commissioned. One of the most substantial projects that Blake undertook for Butts was a series of over 100 impressive watercolours on biblical subjects, which may have been intended for insertion into a printed Bible. Butts also commissioned from Blake watercolour designs illustrating poetry by John Milton (pp.84–5), author of the epic poem *Paradise Lost*, and a set of designs based on the biblical Book of Job.

Another noteworthy project commissioned by Butts was a series of twelve large colour prints, which the civil servant purchased from Blake in 1805–6. For these prints, on which he may have begun work as early as 1795, Blake used an experimental technique, beginning with a base colour print on which he layered ink and watercolour to produce a distinctive vibrancy and depth. The best known of the series is the iconic *Newton* (pp.48–9), which shows a youthful nude Isaac Newton seated on a mossy rock, perhaps underwater, and measuring a diagram with compasses or dividers. The picture has been much discussed and is generally thought to be satirical in intent, caricaturing Newton's efforts to contain the richness of the universe using mathematical formulae (Blake, who criticised Newton in his poetry, was an opponent of overly rigid scientific principles). The image was later picked up by Eduardo Paolozzi for a sculpture displayed outside the British Library in London, where it appears more as a heroic celebration of knowledge than Blake perhaps intended. A bronze cast of the model for the sculpture, made to show the Library Committee, is held in the Tate collection (opposite).

COURTING ARTISTIC SUCCESS

Despite these successful projects, the early nineteenth century also brought further disappointments. In late 1805, Blake was contacted by the Yorkshire publisher Robert Hartley Cromek to execute designs for an edition of Robert Blair's 1743 poem *The Grave*. Blake produced twenty preparatory watercolours for the project; Cromek took these to the Royal Academy, where a large list of subscribers was formed from the Academy's ranks – an unprecedented endorsement of Blake's work from the art establishment. However, apparently without consulting Blake, Cromek gave the task of engraving the final designs to another engraver, Luigi Schiavonetti, whose style was more refined according to the fashion of the day.

Embittered, Blake resolved to take matters into his own hands by initiating his own artistic undertakings. He produced a painting depicting a scene from Geoffrey Chaucer's medieval poem *The Canterbury Tales*, which became the centrepiece of his 1809 'one man show' – a solo exhibition displayed upstairs from the Blake family's hosiery shop at 28 Broad Street. At the heart of the exhibition he placed a print based on the *Canterbury Pilgrims* painting, which was the largest print he ever produced (pp.66–7). But this artwork and the 1809 show were both met with crushing setbacks. Around the same time Blake was working on his *Canterbury Pilgrims*, Cromek commissioned Thomas Stothard to produce a painting of the same subject, and it was Stothard's painting, engraved by Schiavonetti, that won the day, garnering the acclaim that accordingly eluded Blake. In the *Descriptive Catalogue* that accompanied the 1809 exhibition, Blake defended his vision. He felt that his version excelled in its clarity and detail, enabled by strong outlines, whereas Stothard's version suffered from the 'blotting and blurring' quality Blake associated with fashionable oil painting.[23]

In his exhibition, Blake also displayed paintings for which he had used an experimental tempera medium, including his two companion paintings *The Spiritual Form of Nelson Guiding Leviathan* c.1805–9 (p.62) and *The Spiritual Form of Pitt Guiding Behemoth* c.1805 (p.63). These paintings, depicting the naval leader Horatio Nelson and the then British prime minister William Pitt respectively, use apocalyptic imagery drawn from the biblical *Book of Revelation*, and are highly ambiguous: are they celebrating two national heroes, or criticising them through association with violence and apocalypse? In the *Descriptive Catalogue*, Blake advertised his wish to accept 'a national commission to execute these two Pictures' on a scale of 'one hundred feet in height', 'suitable to the grandeur of the nation'.[24] This reveals the grandeur of his own ambitions, though Blake never ended up producing paintings on the scale described.

Blake's 1809 show was a disastrous flop. It was notoriously ill-attended and was reviewed in the journal *The Examiner* as 'a farrago of nonsense, unintelligibleness, egregious vanity', with the artist derided as 'an unfortunate lunatic'.[25] Blake would go on to exhibit some watercolours, and to re-exhibit *Pitt* and *Nelson*, at the Associated Artists in Water Colours exhibition at 16 Old Bond Street in 1812. The society was dissolved soon after due to failing finances. This was the last time Blake exhibited his work.

LATE ILLUMINATED BOOKS

I write in South Molton Street, what I both see and hear
In regions of Humanity, in Londons opening streets.[26]

Blake's devastating failure to achieve public acclaim for his art did not deter him from continuing work on his independent books. In the early nineteenth century, Blake and Catherine – now living in South Molton Street, Mayfair – undertook sporadic reprintings of the earlier books. Blake also worked on proofs for new projects, books entitled *Jerusalem: The Emanation of The Giant Albion* and *Milton: A Poem in 2 Books*. These newer books were highly complex, labyrinthine productions that continue to baffle and intrigue readers today. The highly detailed and finished designs that energise the books represent the culmination of Blake's technical skill in relief etching.

Jerusalem, Blake's last illuminated book, begins with a full-page picture showing a youthful figure, probably the male character named 'Los' in Blake's mythology, stepping through a darkened doorway (p.65). The figure clasps an orb or disc

'Milton a Poem' plate 40
(Copy D) composed
c.1804–11, printed 1818
Relief and white-line
etching with hand-
colouring on paper
Plates range between
13.5 × 9.6 and 16.9 × 12

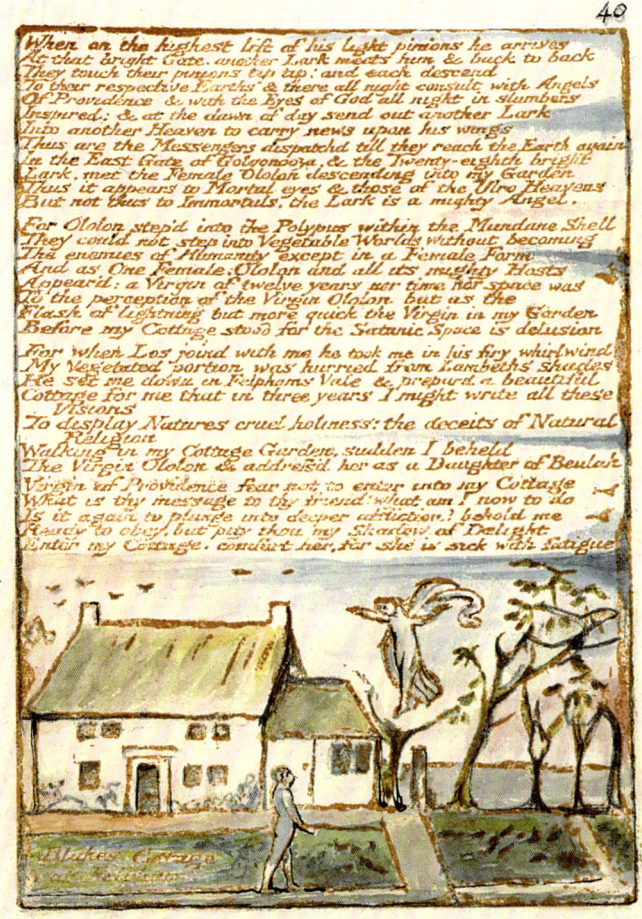

that radiates light out to the picture's margins, lighting the way
on this journey into the mysterious interiors that lie ahead.
This artwork invites us, as readers and viewers, to step inside
the vast universe of Blake's mythology. The journey through the
'dark mazes' of Blake's poetry and art is often as arduous as it
is fascinating, but the world of Blake's late books, *Milton* and
Jerusalem, is also a familiar world, one built on the foundation
of London, where Blake lived and worked for almost all his life.

In his home city of London, Blake hoped for the 'New
Jerusalem', a kind of earthly paradise prophesied in the Bible,
to be restored. Readers may be familiar with the hymn
'Jerusalem', as set to music by Hubert Parry in 1916, the lyrics

for which come from Blake's illuminated book *Milton*. The hymn is often sung in a patriotic spirit, but the wording is actually rather pessimistic: Blake questions the notion that any holy land, or 'Jerusalem', could ever have been 'builded here' among the 'dark Satanic Mills' of industrial Britain. Blake's books *Jerusalem* and *Milton* try to light the way to a restored or rebuilt version of this lost utopia, but Blake constantly moves between optimism and pessimism when addressing the social and political structures of his day.

THE 1820s: BLAKE'S LAST YEARS

In 1821 Blake and Catherine moved to 3 Fountain Court, off the Strand, where they would live until Blake's death. During these final years Blake lived in relative obscurity and poverty, but he did have some friends and supporters, especially the artist John Linnell. He also amassed a small group of followers who called themselves 'the Ancients' because they wanted to restore a pristine version of art, often drawing on medieval models. The principal members of the Ancients group – a precursor to the slightly later artistic 'brotherhood' known as the Pre-Raphaelites – were Samuel Palmer, George Richmond and Edward Calvert, artists who admired Blake's work for its visionary qualities and themes of innocence and spirituality.

During this time, Linnell was Blake's most consistent patron. He commissioned important works from Blake, including a set of designs to *The Book of Job* (1821) and a major series of designs to Dante's *Divine Comedy*, on which Blake was working during the final years of his life (1824–7). Blake produced 102 ambitious and vibrant watercolours for this series, which were left in varying states of completion at the time of his death, only seven of them engraved. At the same time, Blake was also at work on a series of designs to John Bunyan's seventeenth-century text *The Pilgrim's Progress*, which Catherine may have continued working on after his death.[27]

John Linnell also introduced Blake to other important contacts, including Dr Robert John Thornton, who commissioned from Blake a series of woodcut designs for an edition of his book *The Pastorals of Virgil* (1821). The pastoral simplicity of the resulting prints, gloomy and charming in equal measure, inspired the art of the Ancients: the clearest parallels can be found in Edward Calvert's woodcuts, which closely follow Blake's model.

Through Linnell, Blake also met John Varley, a water-colourist and astrologer who took an interest in Blake's claims of experiencing 'visions'. Blake apparently saw such visions in Varley's presence on several occasions, transposing these into sketches known as the 'Visionary Heads'. One of these visions was the inspiration for Blake's famous painting *The Ghost of a Flea* (p.71) (the image appears on the reverse of a postcard sent by Hannibal Lecter in Ridley Scott's 2001 film *Hannibal*). Linnell eventually engraved several of the drawings Blake made of these 'Visionary Heads' for Varley's *Treatise on Zodiacal Physiognomy*, published in 1828, the year after Blake died.

In 1826, Blake fell ill with a disease from which he would never fully recover. His letters from the final year of his life record 'Shivring Fits' and a feeling of being 'an Old Man feeble & tottering'.[28] Even while bedridden, Blake continued to work on his art: Samuel Palmer reported finding him 'sixty-seven years old, but hard working on a bed covered with books… like one of the Antique patriarchs, or a dying Michael Angelo'.[29] Technical analysis of one of the Dante designs, held at the National Gallery of Victoria, revealed a small feather embedded in the layers of paint, which may have come from Blake's bedsheets.[30] Even until his last days, then, Blake remained dedicated to his art. He died at his home at Fountain Court on 12 August 1827, with Catherine by his side. Catherine would go on to live until 18 October 1831.

The Blakes were buried separately and in unmarked graves at Bunhill Fields, a burial ground intended for Dissenters (Protestant Christians who broke away from the Church of England). In 2018, the Blake Society unveiled a new headstone marking the precise spot where William Blake lies. It is inscribed with the following lines from Blake's *Jerusalem*:

I give you the end of a golden string,
Only wind it into a ball:
It will lead you in at Heavens gate,
Built in Jerusalem's wall.[31]

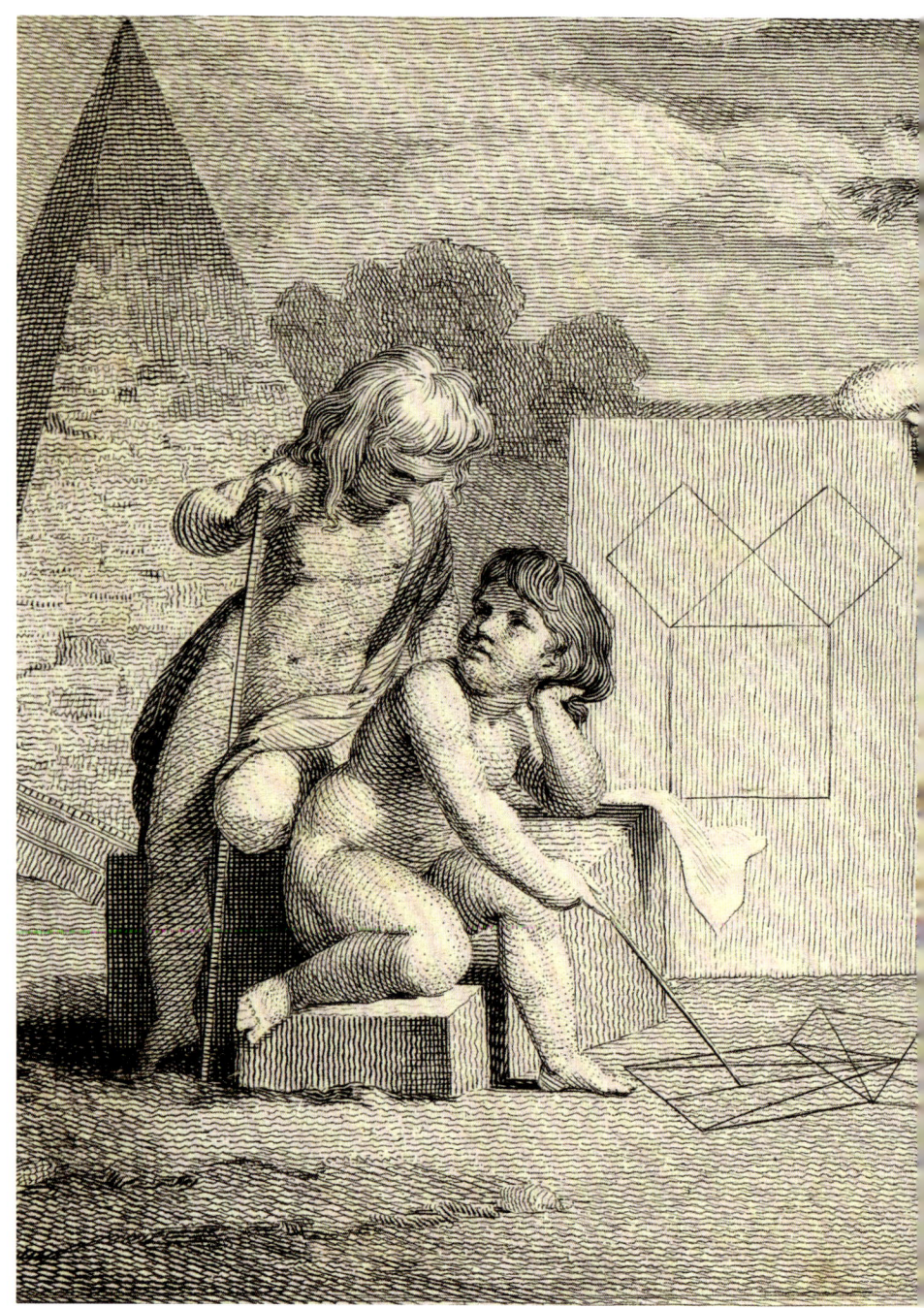

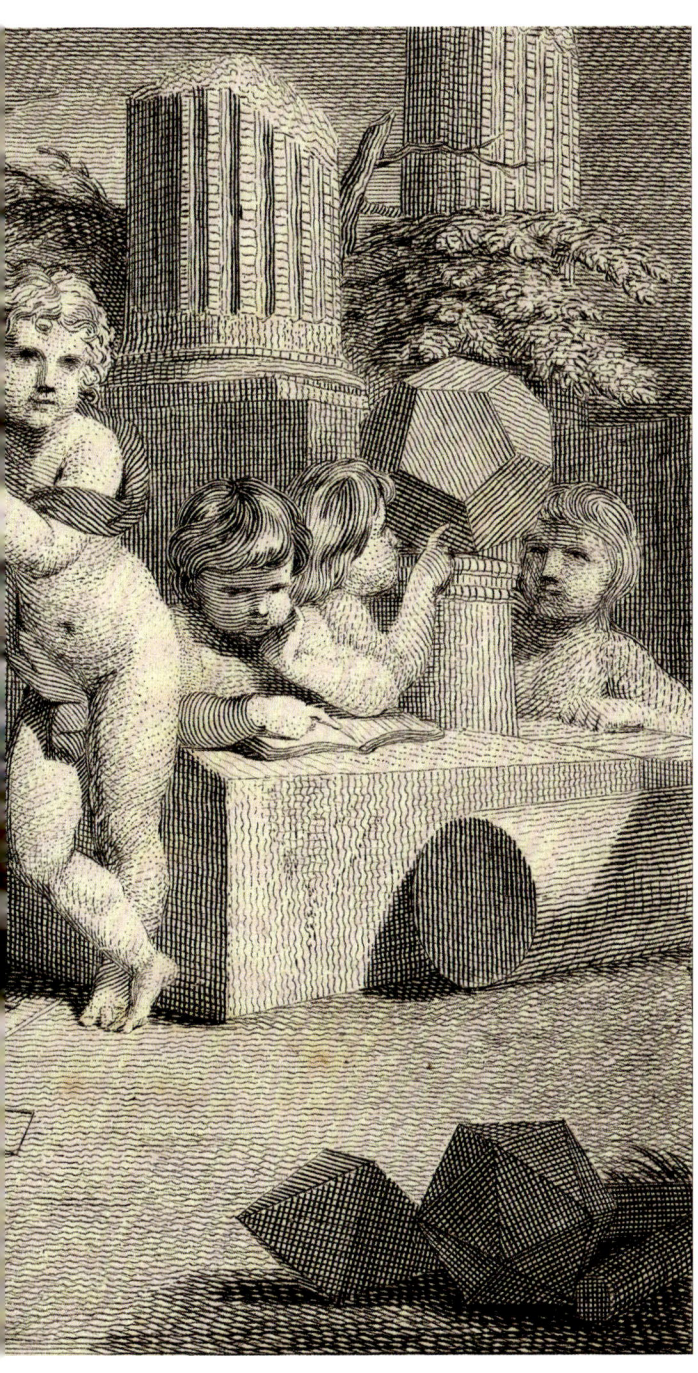

William Blake
after Thomas Stothard
*Vignette for Bonnycastle's
'Introduction to Mensuration'*
1782; this version is from
1794 edition
Etching and engraving
on paper
7.2 × 9.5

OVERLEAF
*Oberon, Titania and Puck with
Fairies Dancing* c.1785
Graphite and watercolour
on paper
47.5 × 67.5

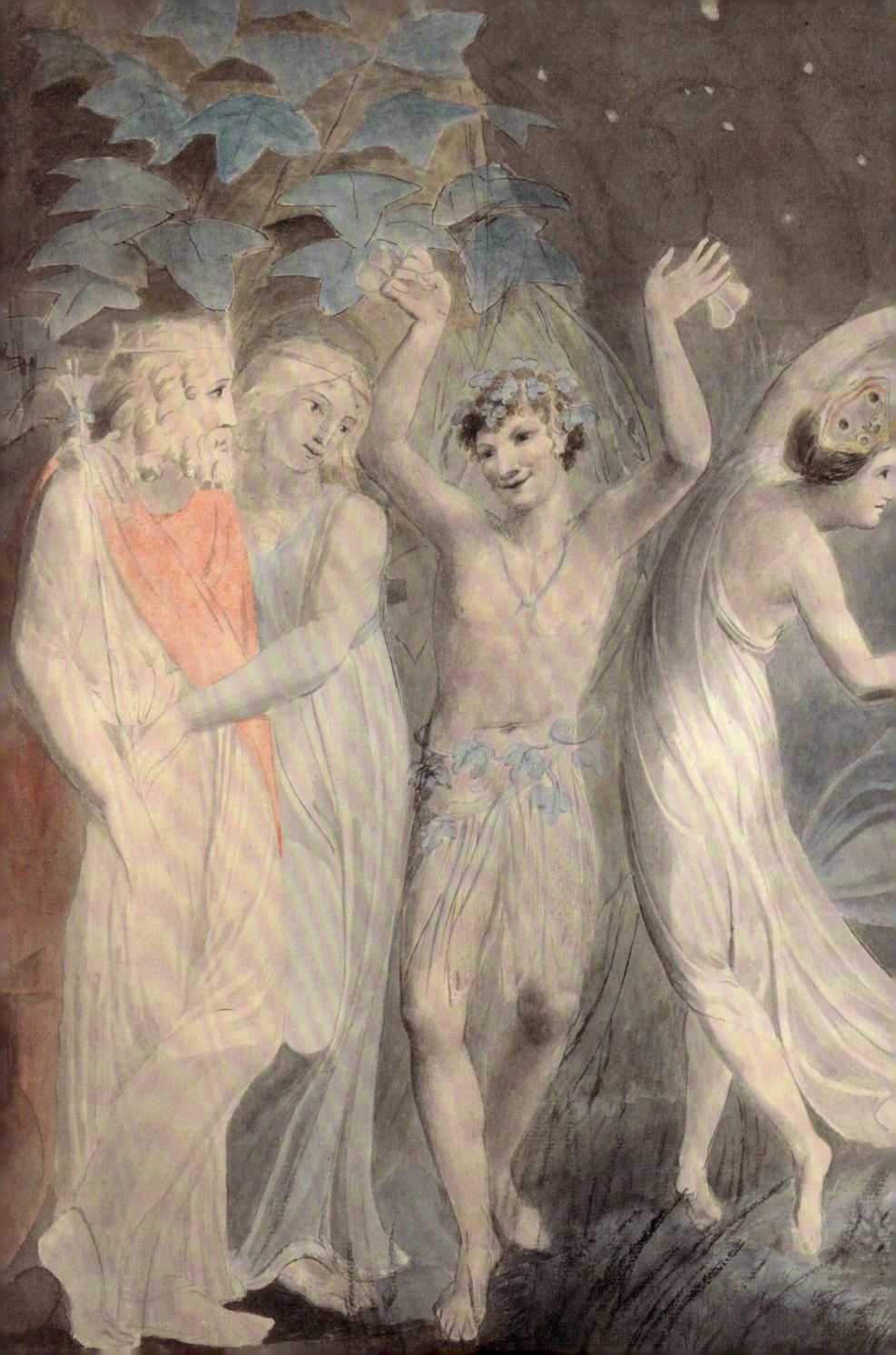

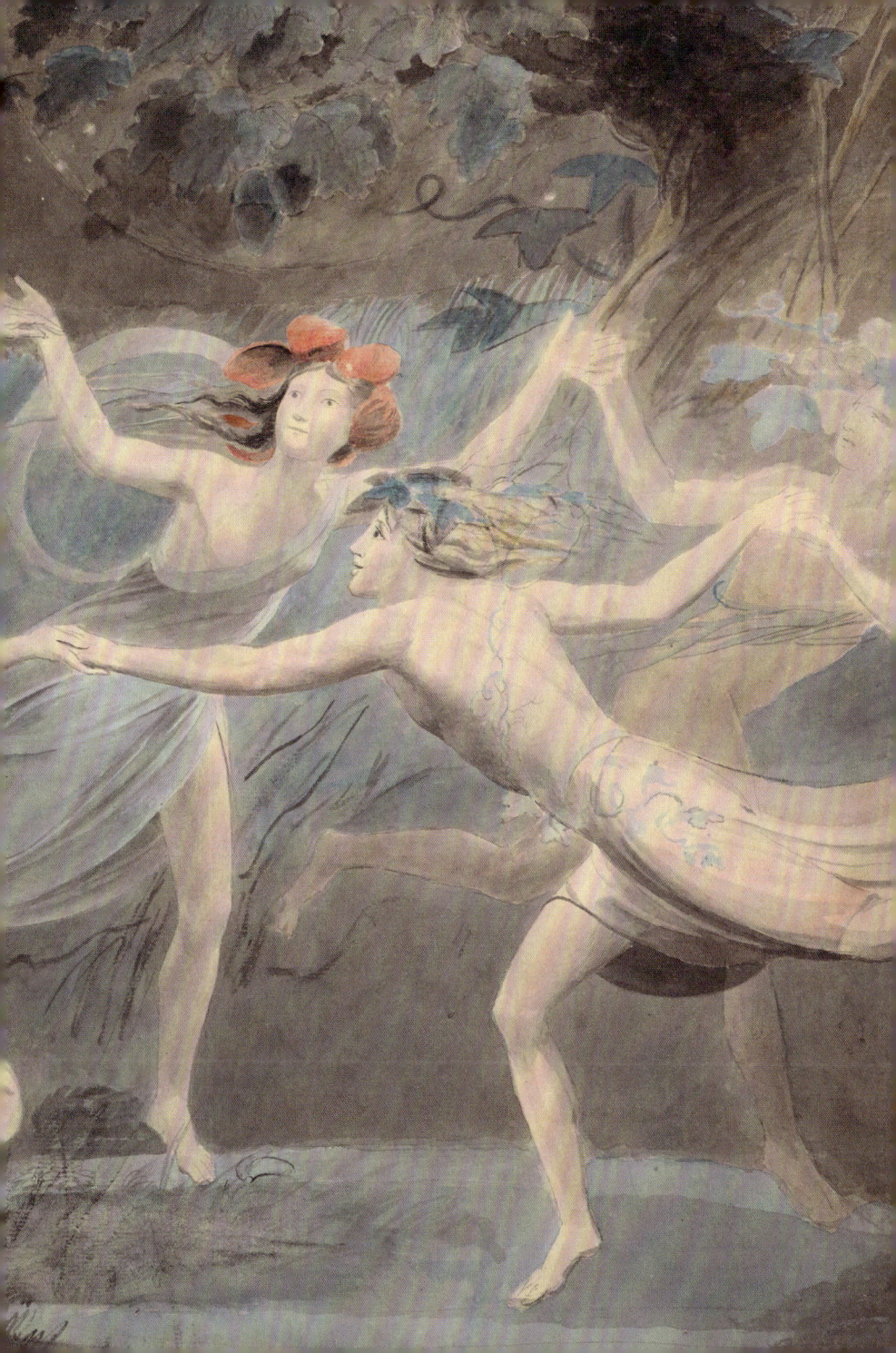

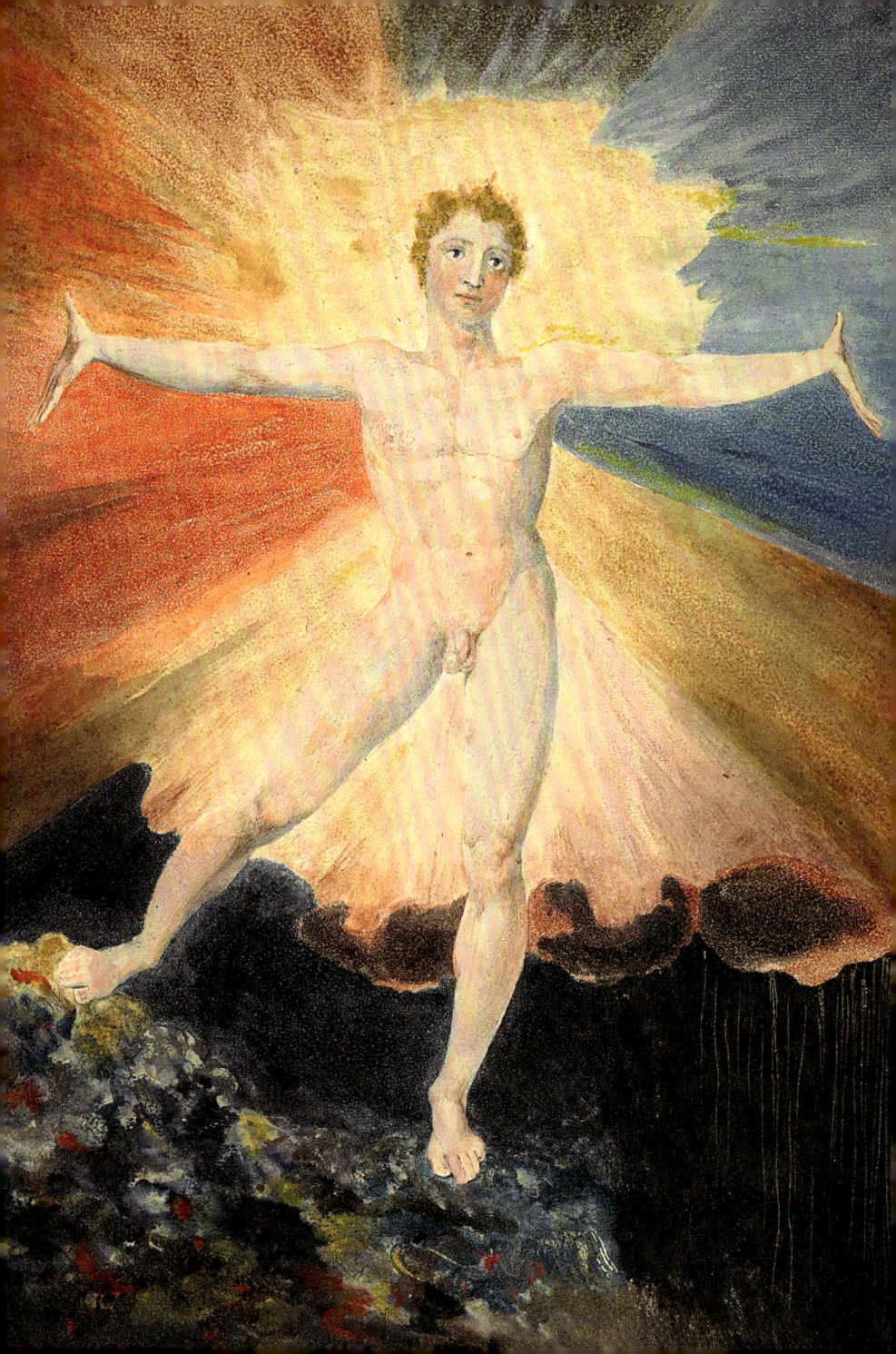

Albion Rose (also known as 'Glad Day') 1794–6
Engraving and hand-colouring on paper
27.2 × 20

after William Blake
'Songs of Innocence': Title-Page
composed 1789, printed 1831 or later
Relief etching on paper
12 × 6.4

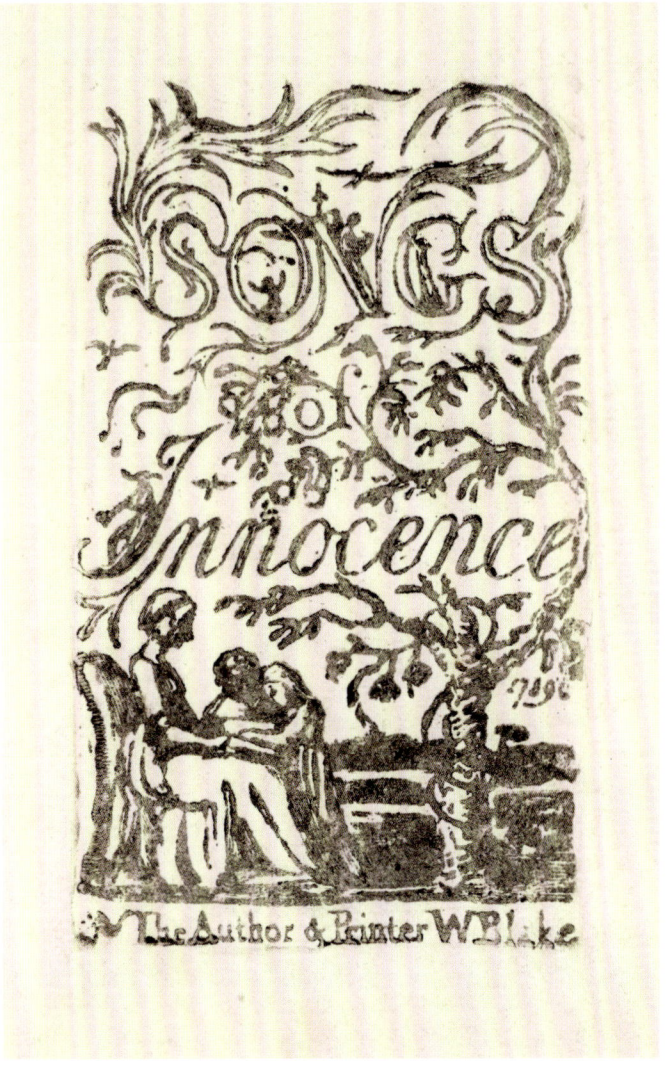

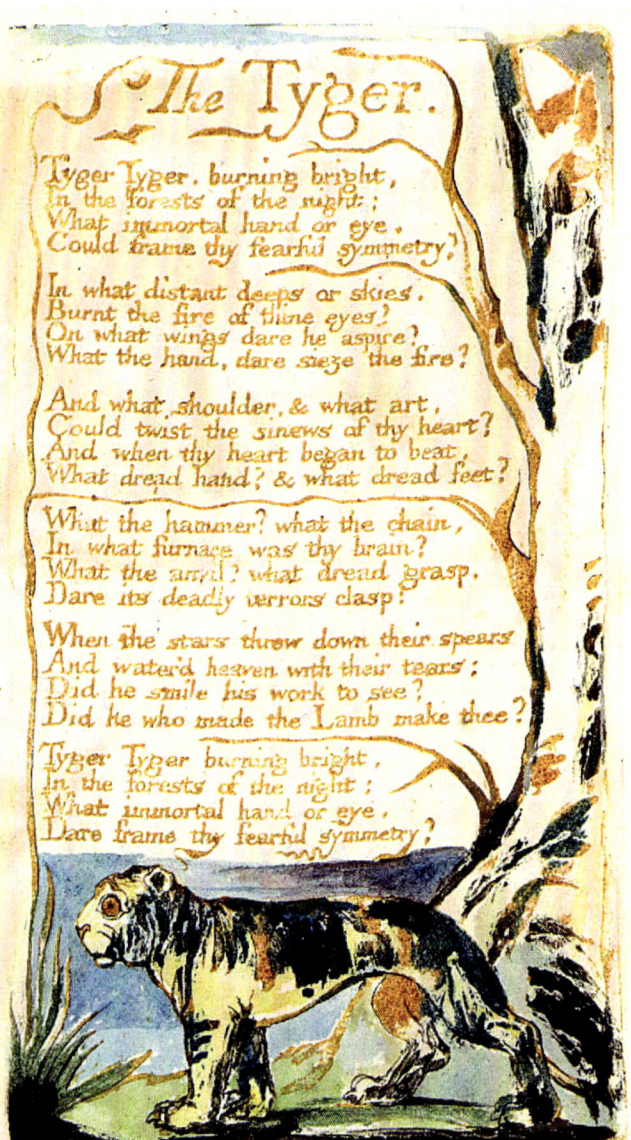

'The Tyger' (from 'Songs of Innocence and of Experience', Copy C) 1794
Relief etching with colour printing and hand-colouring on paper
Plates range between 12.4 × 7.9 and 10.9 × 6.3

'The Lamb' (from 'Songs of Innocence and of Experience', Copy C) 1789
Relief etching with hand-colouring on paper
Plates range between 12.4 × 7.9 and 10.9 × 6.3

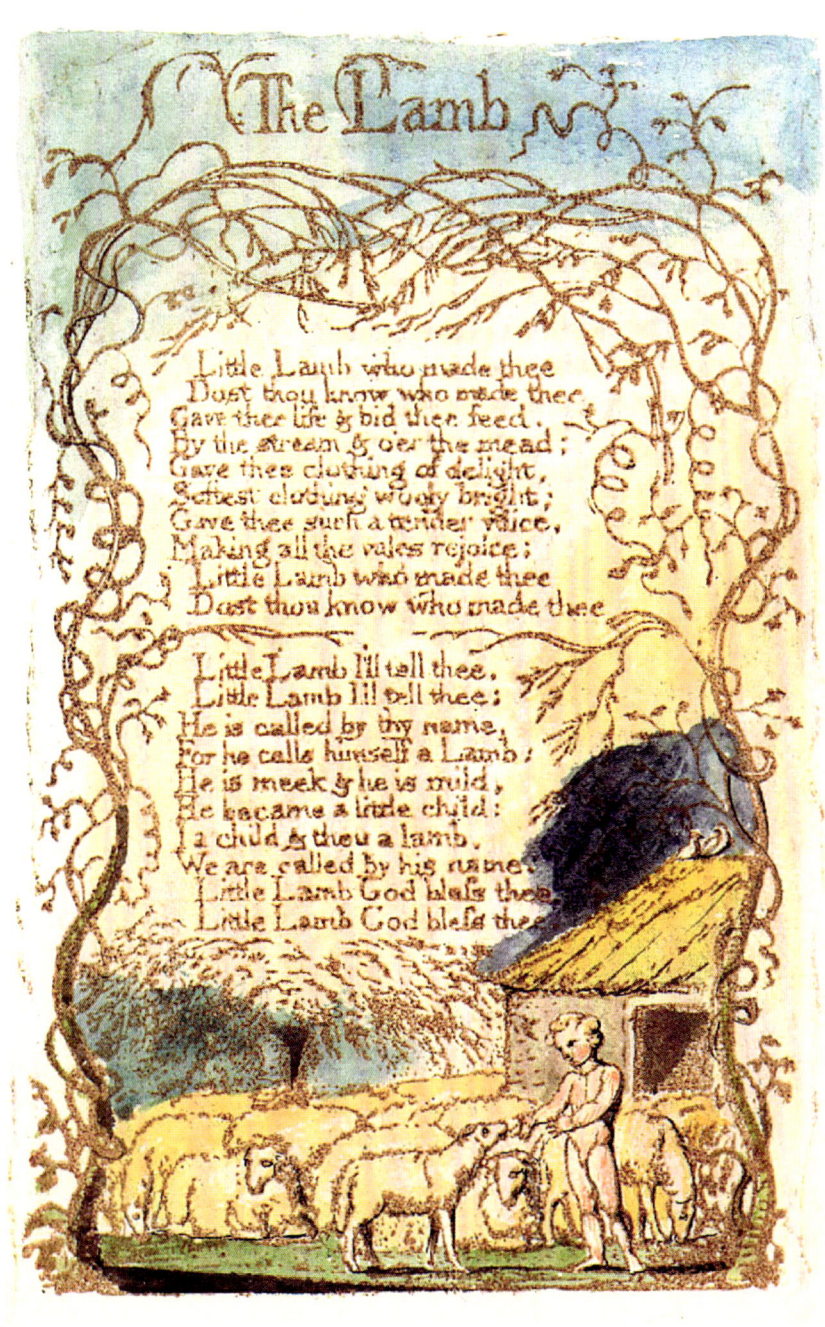

The Lamb

Little Lamb who made thee
Dost thou know who made thee
Gave thee life & bid thee feed.
By the stream & o'er the mead;
Gave thee clothing of delight,
Softest clothing wooly bright;
Gave thee such a tender voice,
Making all the vales rejoice;
    Little Lamb who made thee
    Dost thou know who made thee

Little Lamb I'll tell thee,
Little Lamb I'll tell thee;
He is called by thy name,
For he calls himself a Lamb:
He is meek & he is mild,
He became a little child:
I a child & thou a lamb,
We are called by his name.
    Little Lamb God bless thee
    Little Lamb God bless thee

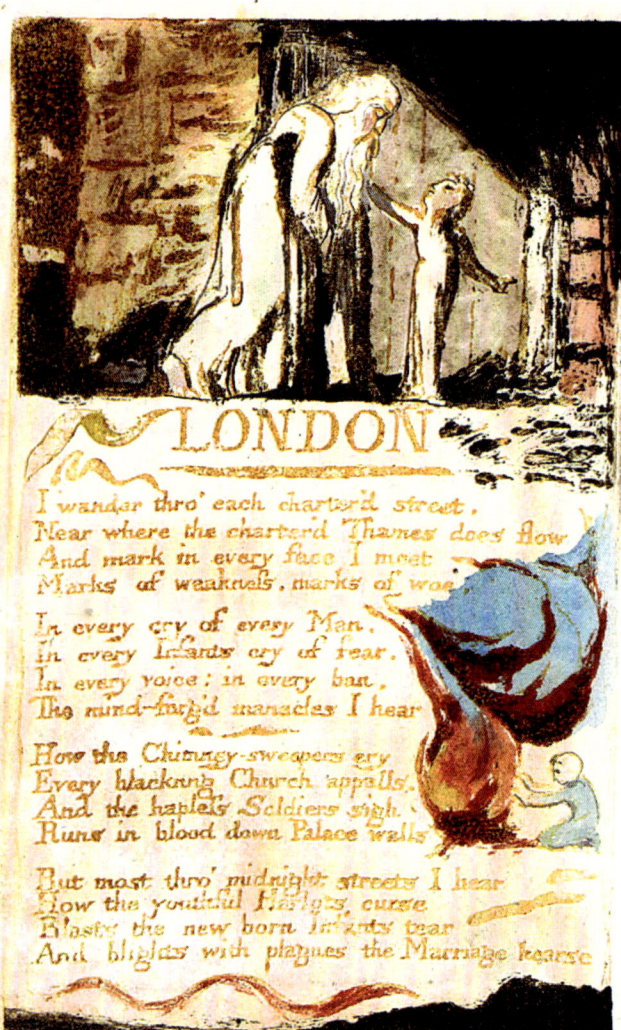

LONDON

I wander thro' each charter'd street,
Near where the charter'd Thames does flow
And mark in every face I meet
Marks of weakness, marks of woe

In every cry of every Man,
In every Infants cry of fear,
In every voice: in every ban,
The mind-forg'd manacles I hear

How the Chimney-sweepers cry
Every blackning Church appalls,
And the hapless Soldiers sigh
Runs in blood down Palace walls

But most thro' midnight streets I hear
How the youthful Harlots curse
Blasts the new born Infants tear
And blights with plagues the Marriage hearse

'London' (from 'Songs of
Innocence and of Experience',
Copy C) 1794
Relief etching with
colour printing and
hand-colouring on paper
Plates range between
12.4 × 7.9 and 10.9 × 6.3

Frontispiece to 'Visions of the
Daughters of Albion' 1796
Relief etching, ink and
watercolour on paper
17 × 12

OVERLEAF
Plate 4 of 'Visions of the
Daughters of Albion' 1796
Relief etching, ink and
watercolour on paper
7.5 × 11.5

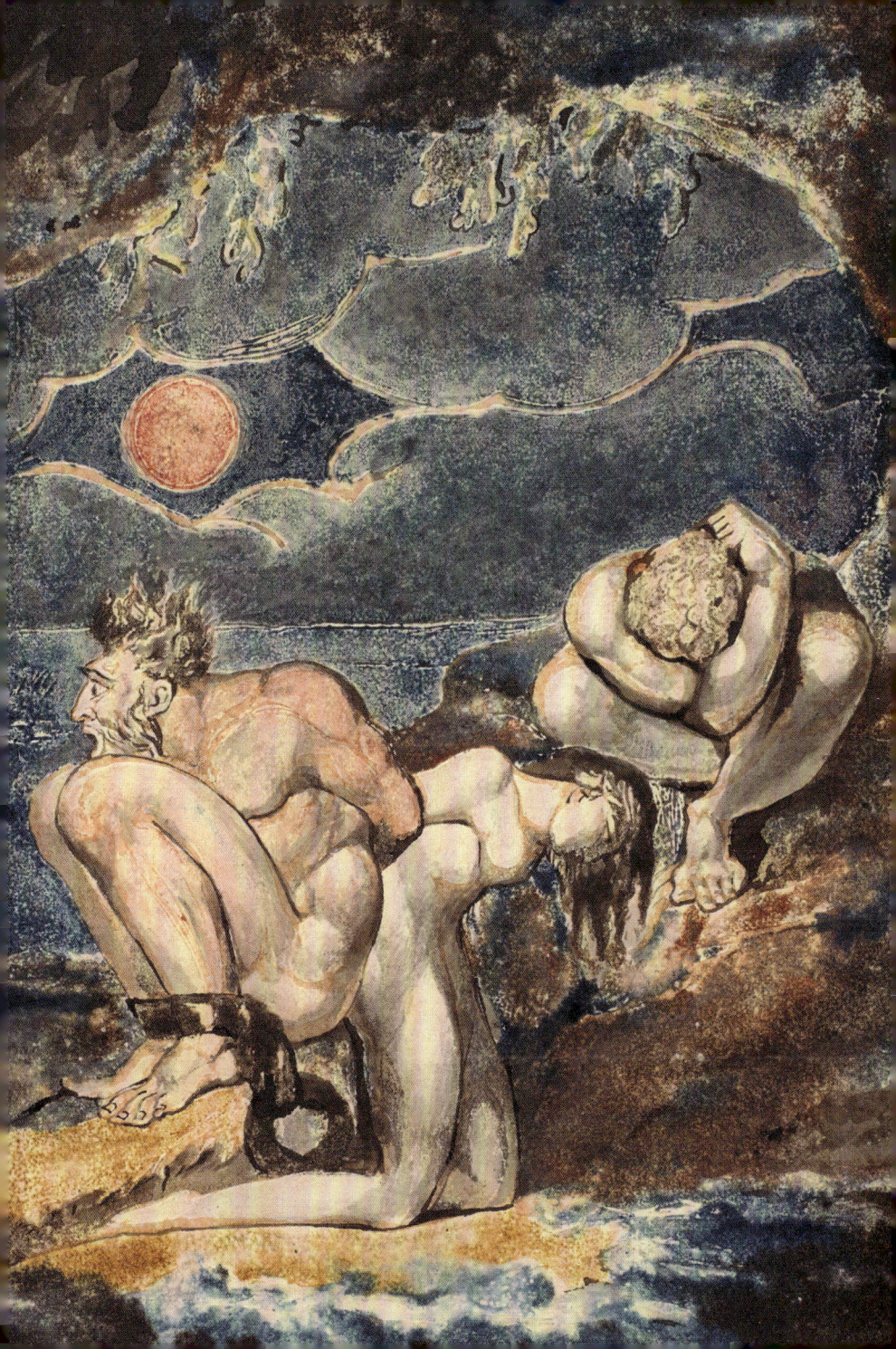

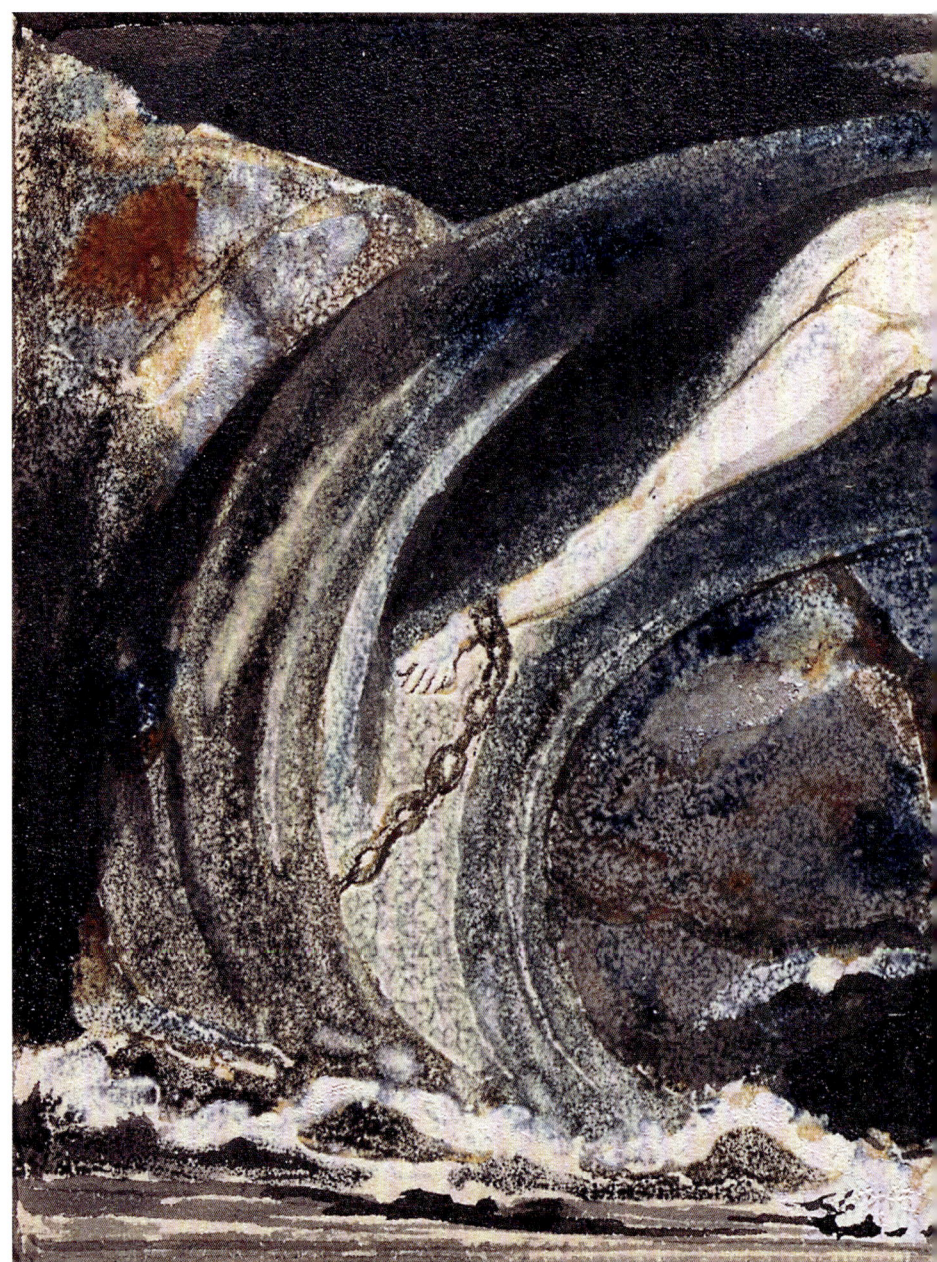

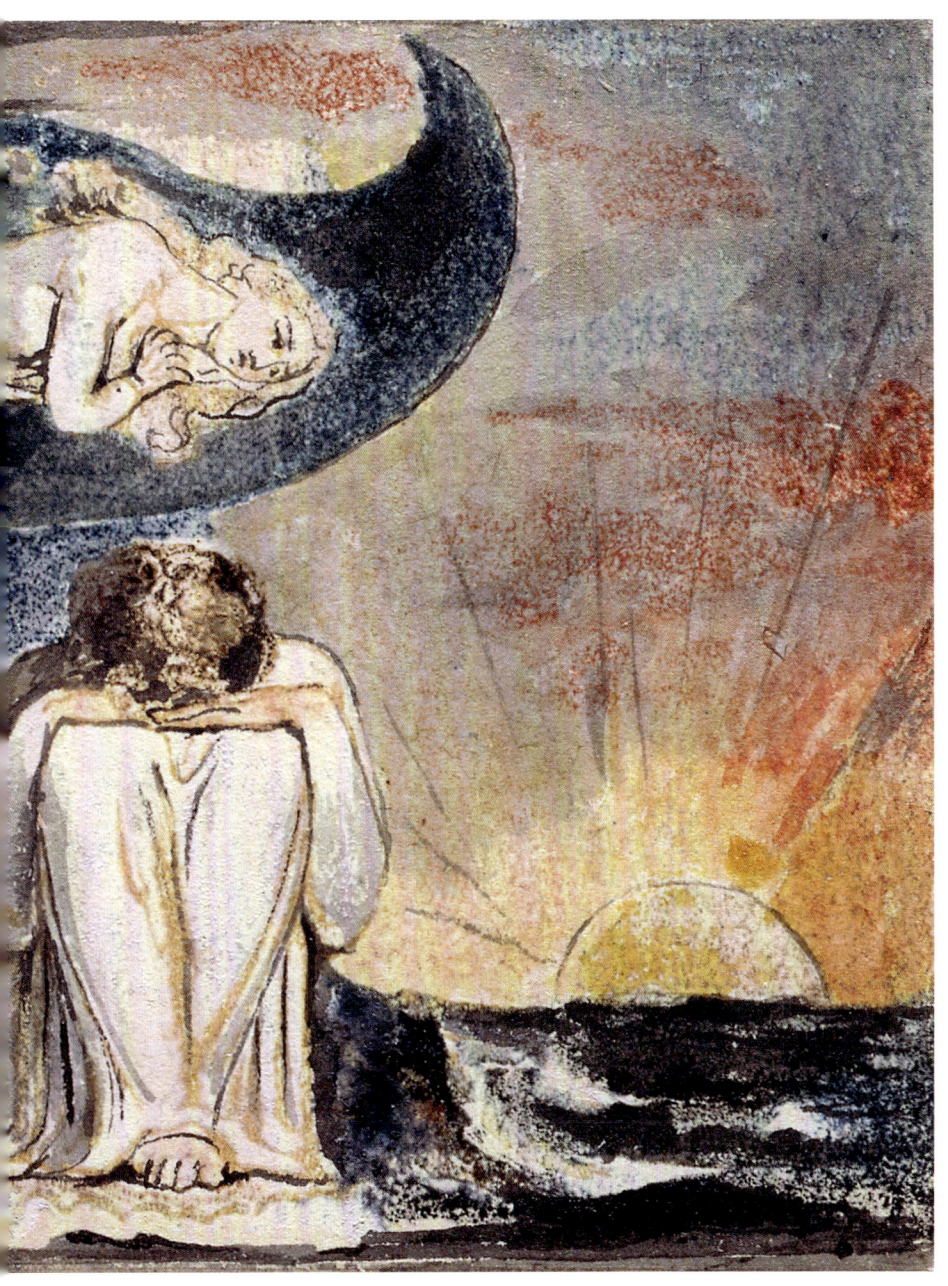

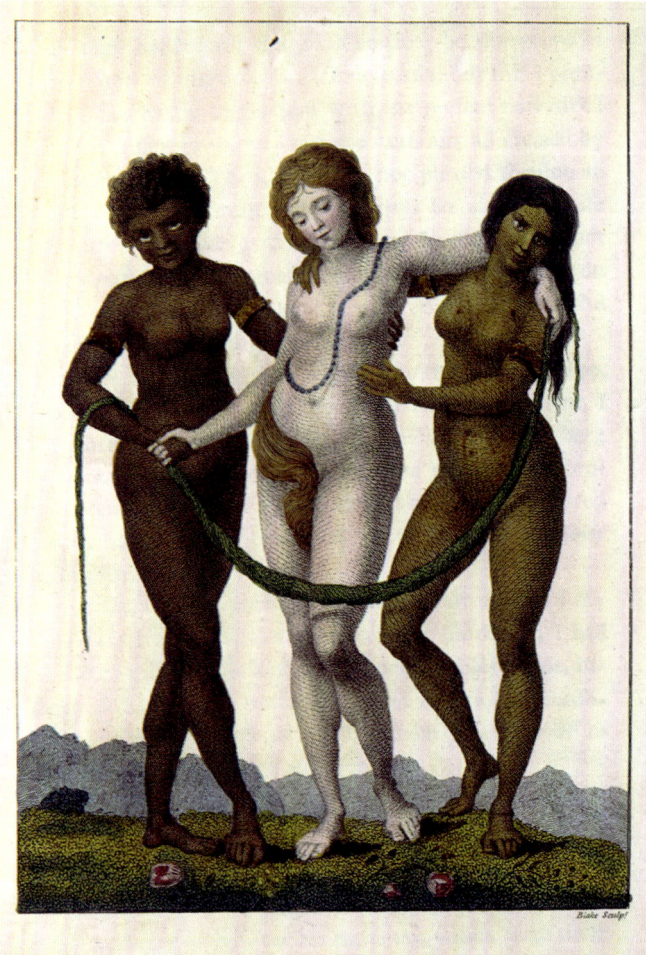

Europe supported by Africa & America.

Blake Sculp.

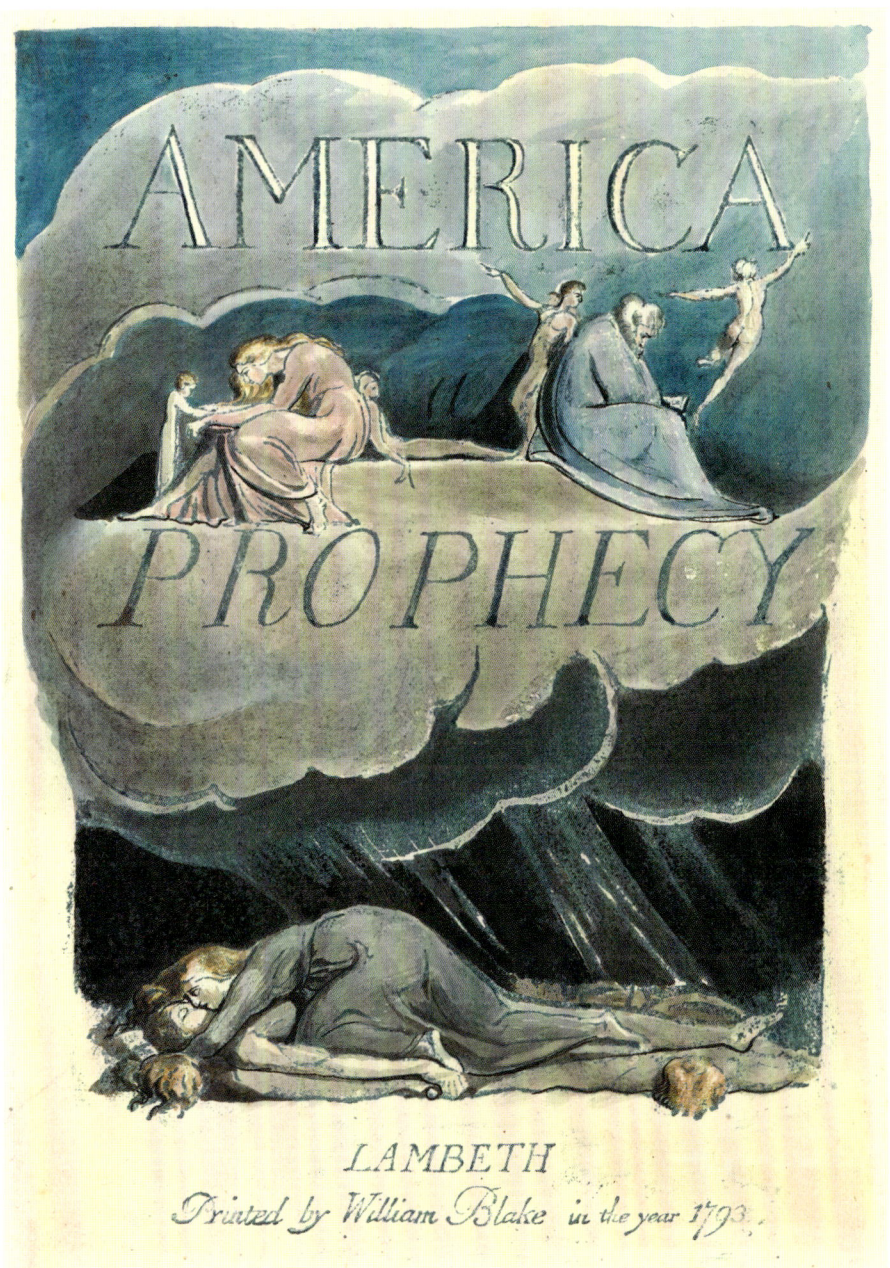

AMERICA

PROPHECY

LAMBETH
Printed by William Blake in the year 1793.

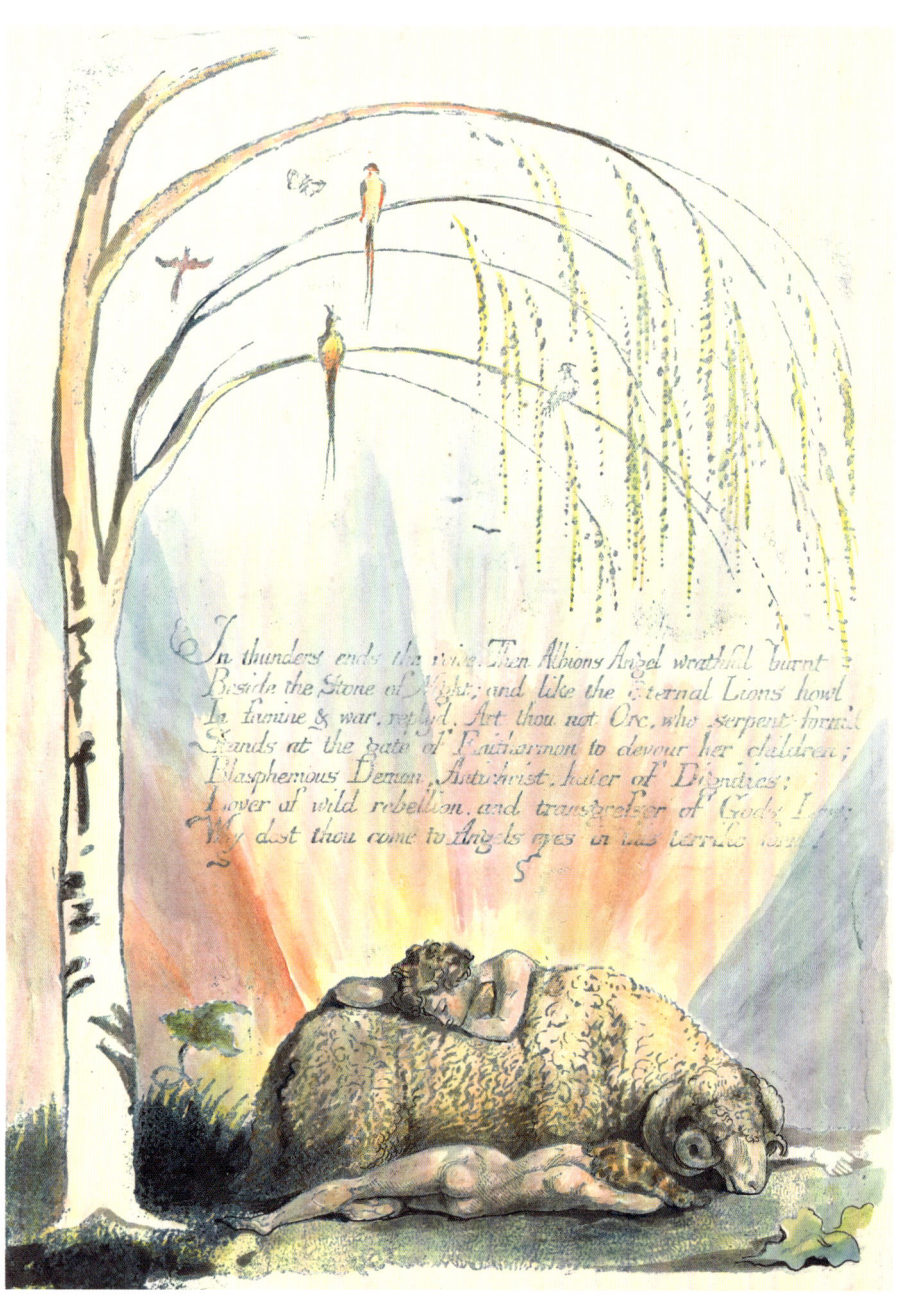

In thunders ends the voice. Then Albions Angel wrathful burnt
Beside the Stone of Night; and like the Eternal Lions howl
In famine & war, reply'd. Art thou not Orc, who serpent-formd
Stands at the gate of Enitharmon to devour her children;
Blasphemous Demon, Antichrist, hater of Dignities;
Lover of wild rebellion, and transgresser of Gods Law;
Why dost thou come to Angels eyes in this terrific form.

'America a Prophecy' plate 7 (Copy M) composed 1793, printed c.1807
Relief with colour printing on paper
Plates range between 23.8 × 17.4 and 23.1 × 16.3

Title-page to 'Europe a Prophecy' (Copy K) composed 1794, printed 1821
Relief etching with extensive hand-colouring on paper
Plates range between 23.9 × 17.3 and 23.1 × 16.4

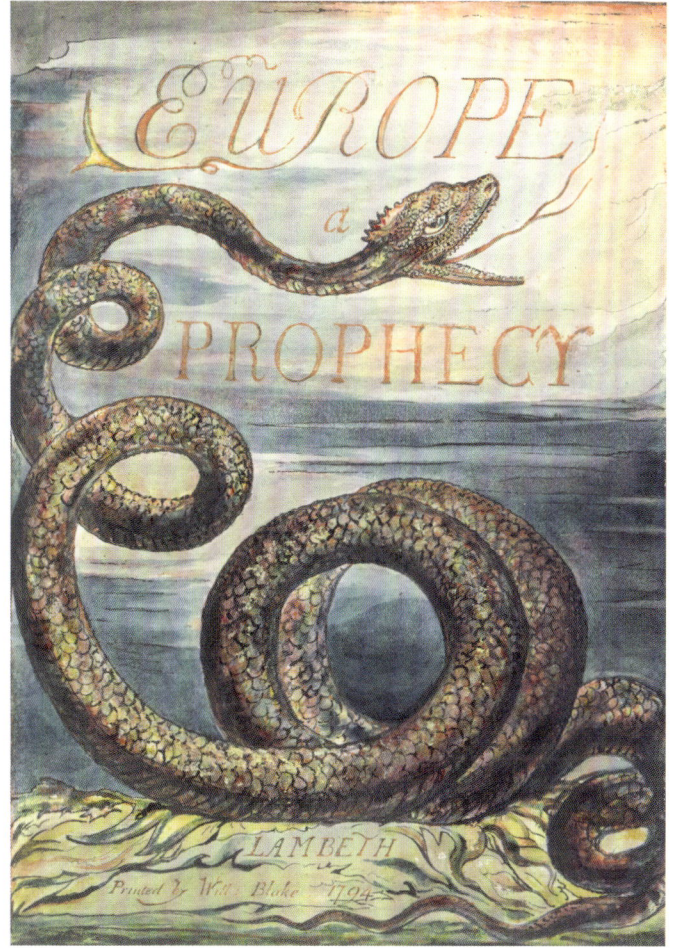

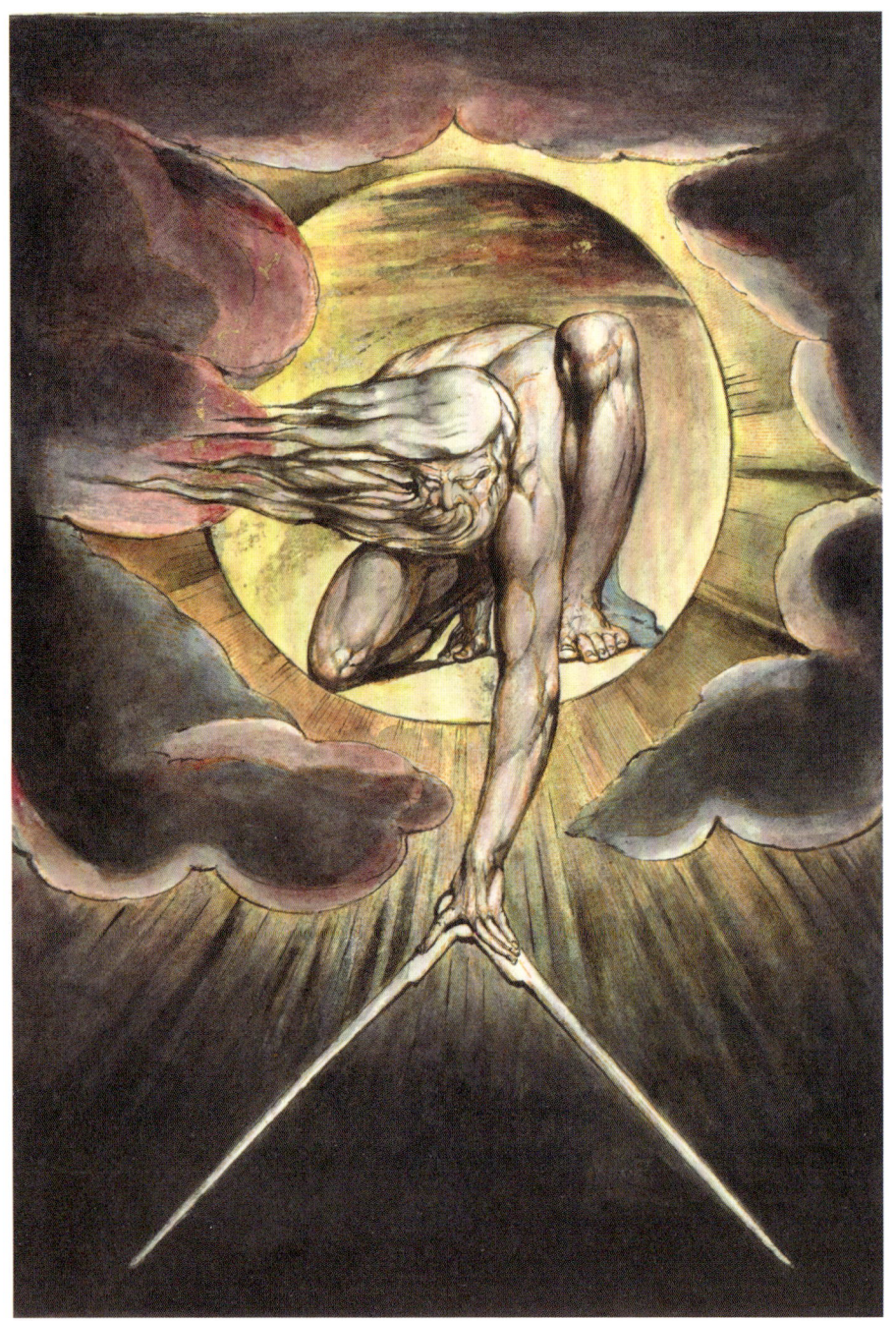

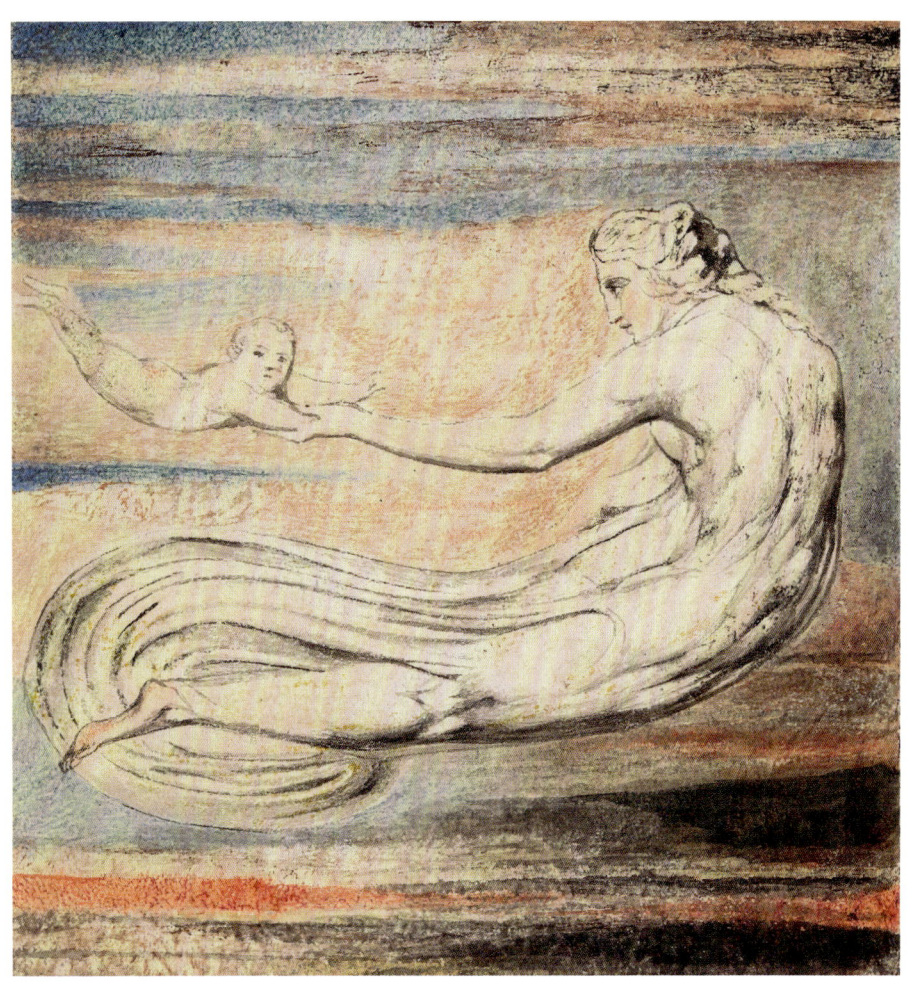

Frontispiece to 'Europe
a Prophecy' (Copy K)
composed 1794, printed
1821
Relief and white-line
etching with extensive
hand-colouring on paper
Plates range between
23.9 × 17.3 and 23.1 × 16.4

'Teach these Souls to Fly' 1796
Design for *The First Book
of Urizen*
Relief etching, ink and
watercolour on paper
10.9 × 10.2

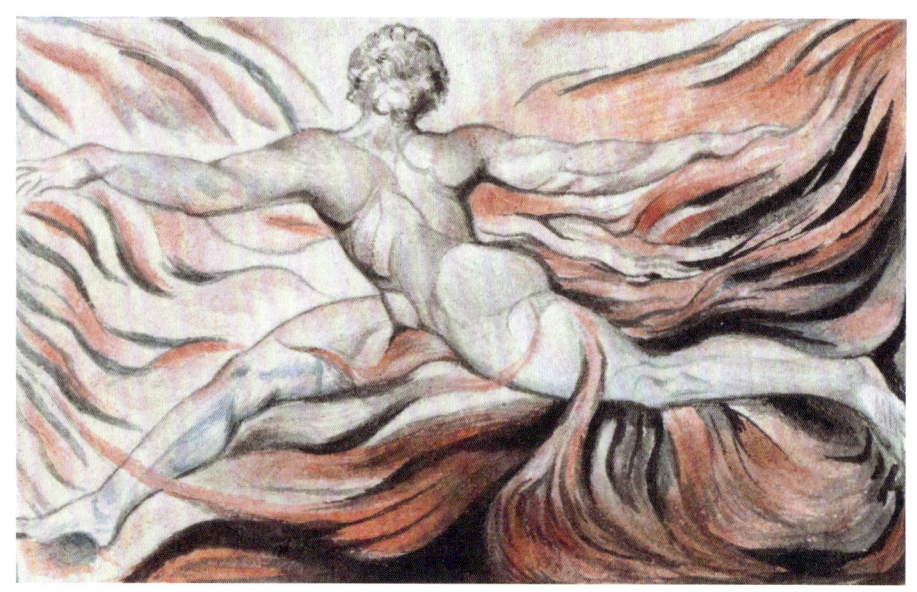

'Oh! Flames of Furious Desires'
1796
Design for The First Book
of Urizen
Watercolour on paper
6 × 9.8

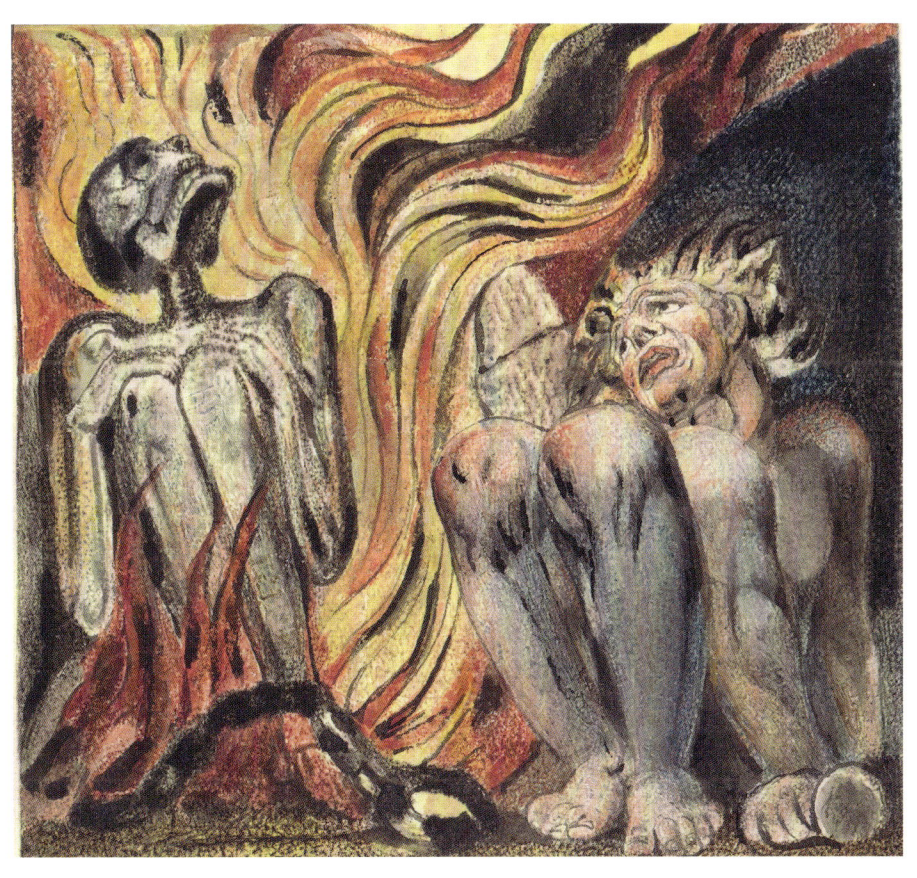

The First Book of Urizen 1796,
c.1818
Etching with paint,
watercolour and ink
on paper
26.6 × 18.5

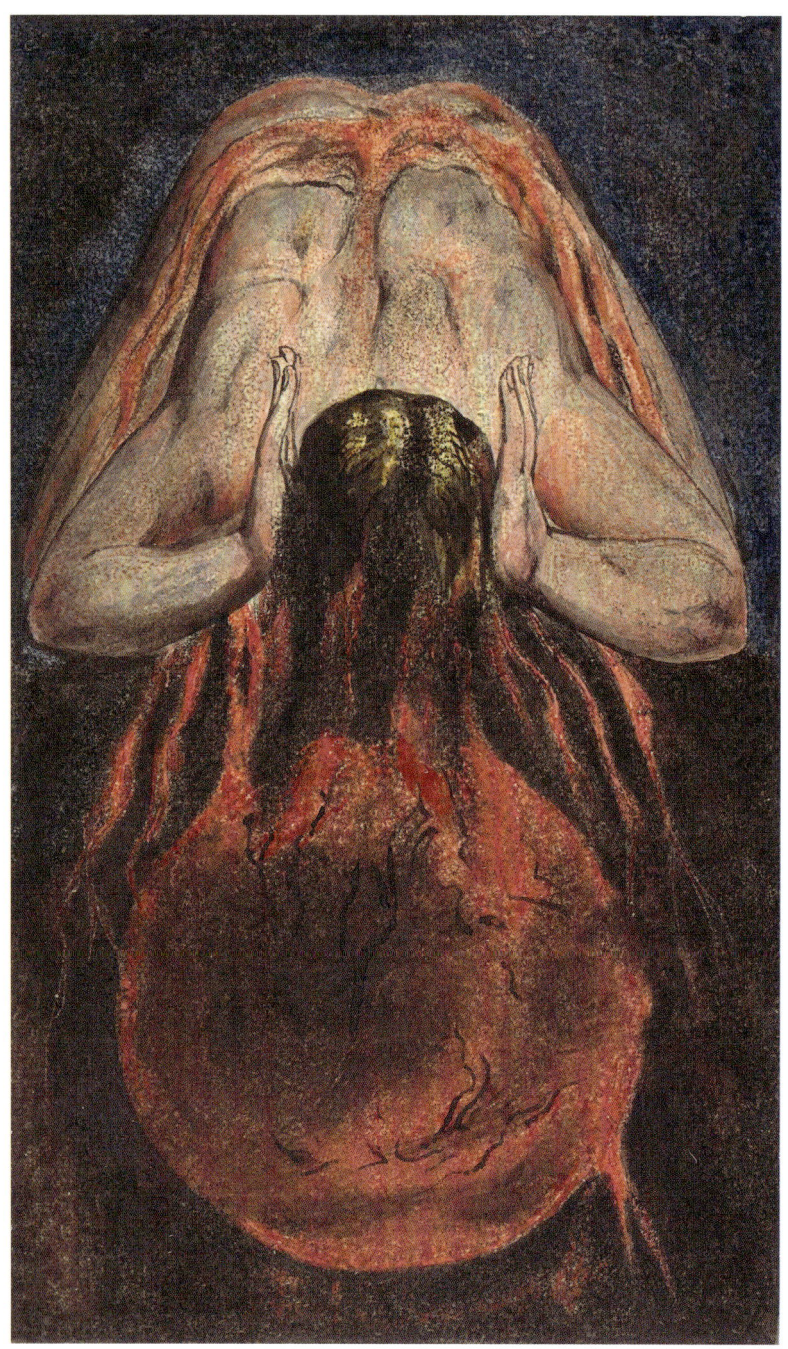

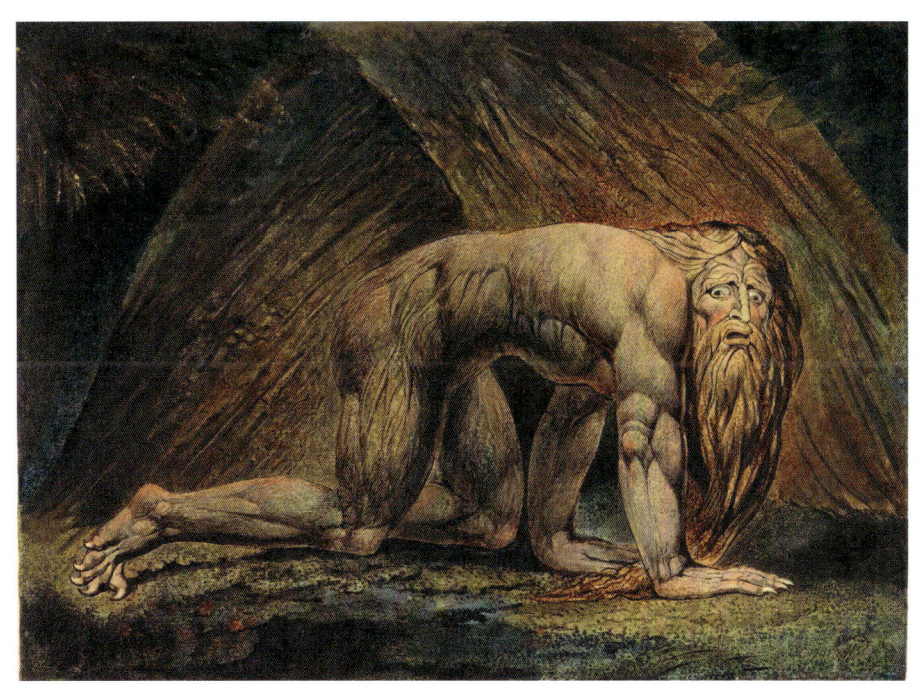

First Book of Urizen pl.15 1796,
c.1818
Etching with paint,
watercolour and ink
on paper
25.9 × 18.2

Nebuchadnezzar 1795–c.1805
Colour print, ink and
watercolour on paper
54.3 × 72.5

OVERLEAF
Newton c.1795–1805
Colour print, ink and
watercolour on paper
46 × 60

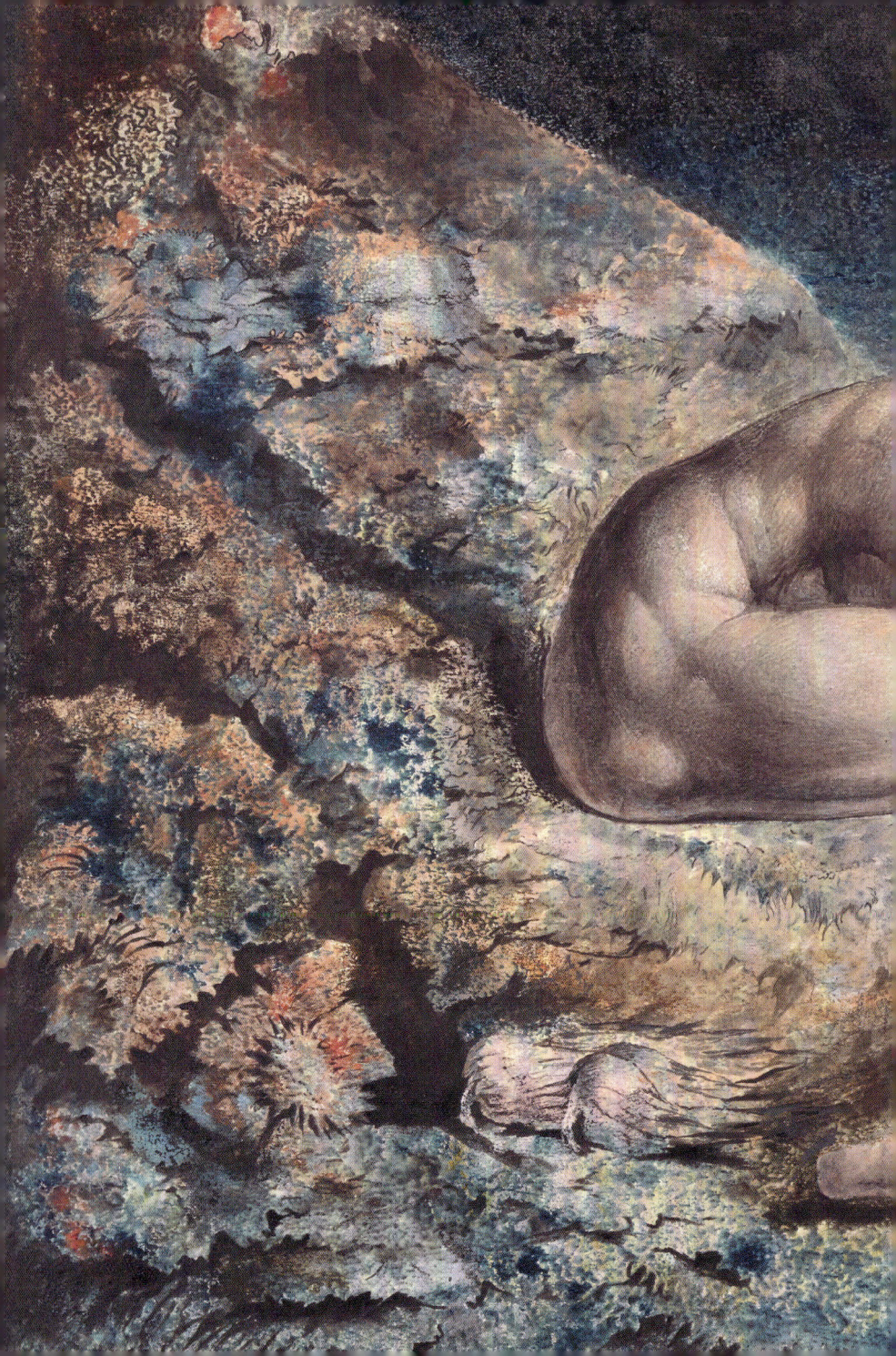

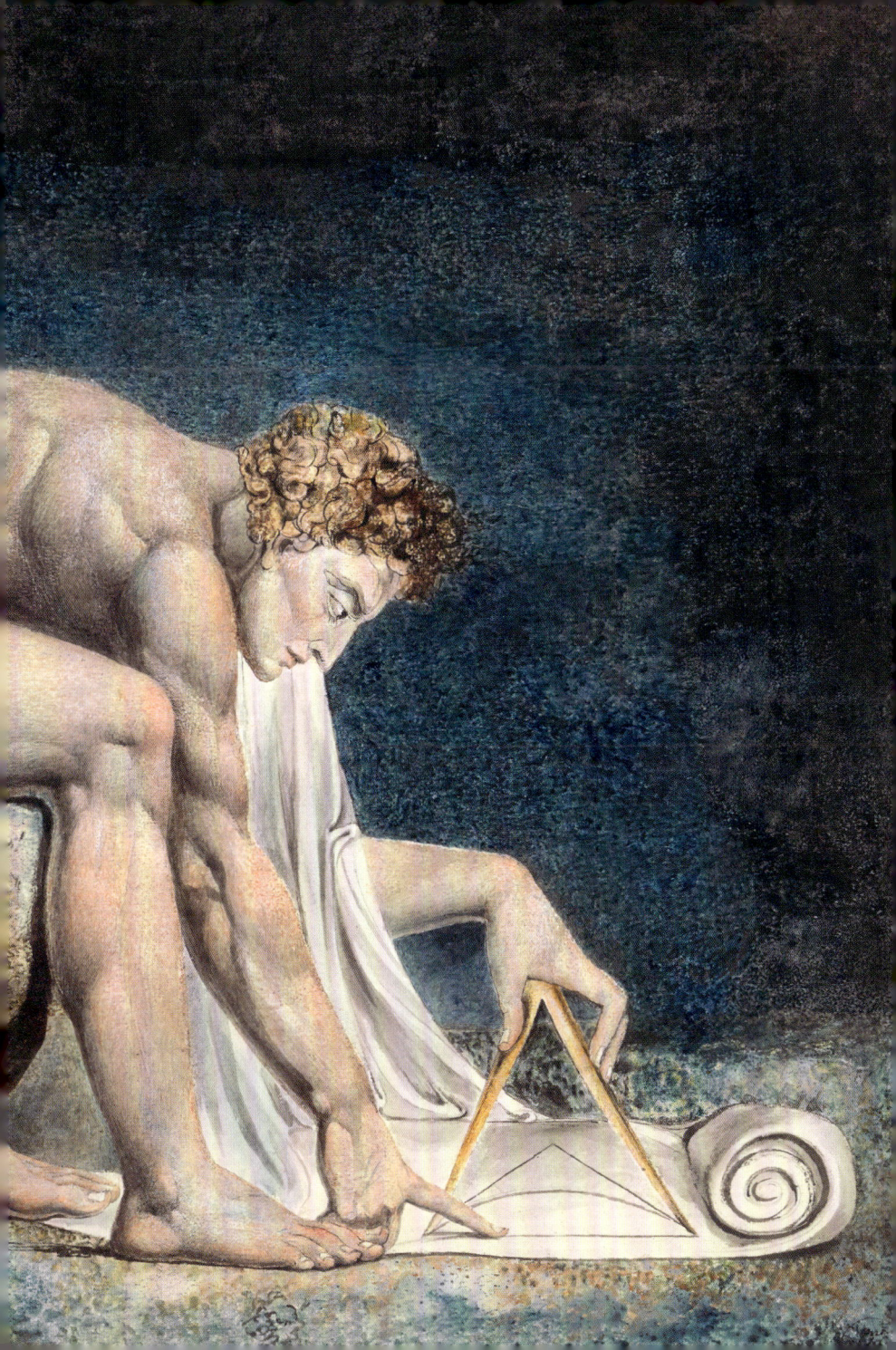

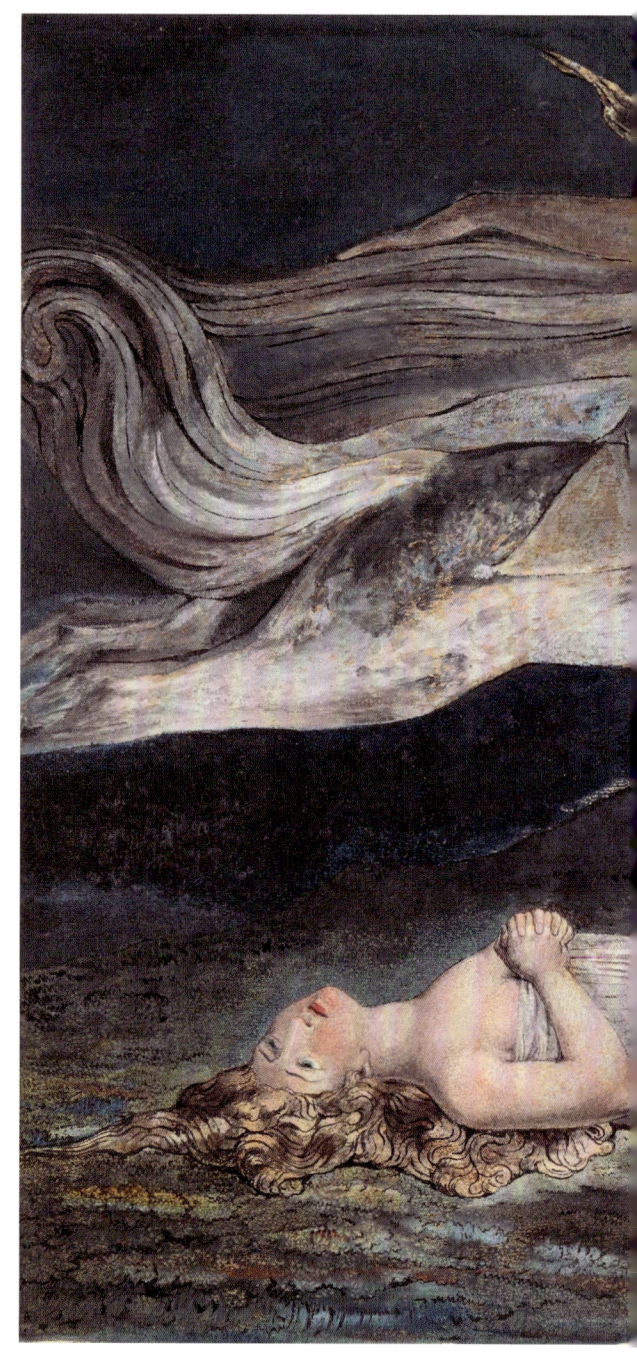

Pity c.1795
Colour print, ink and
watercolour on paper
42.5 × 53.9

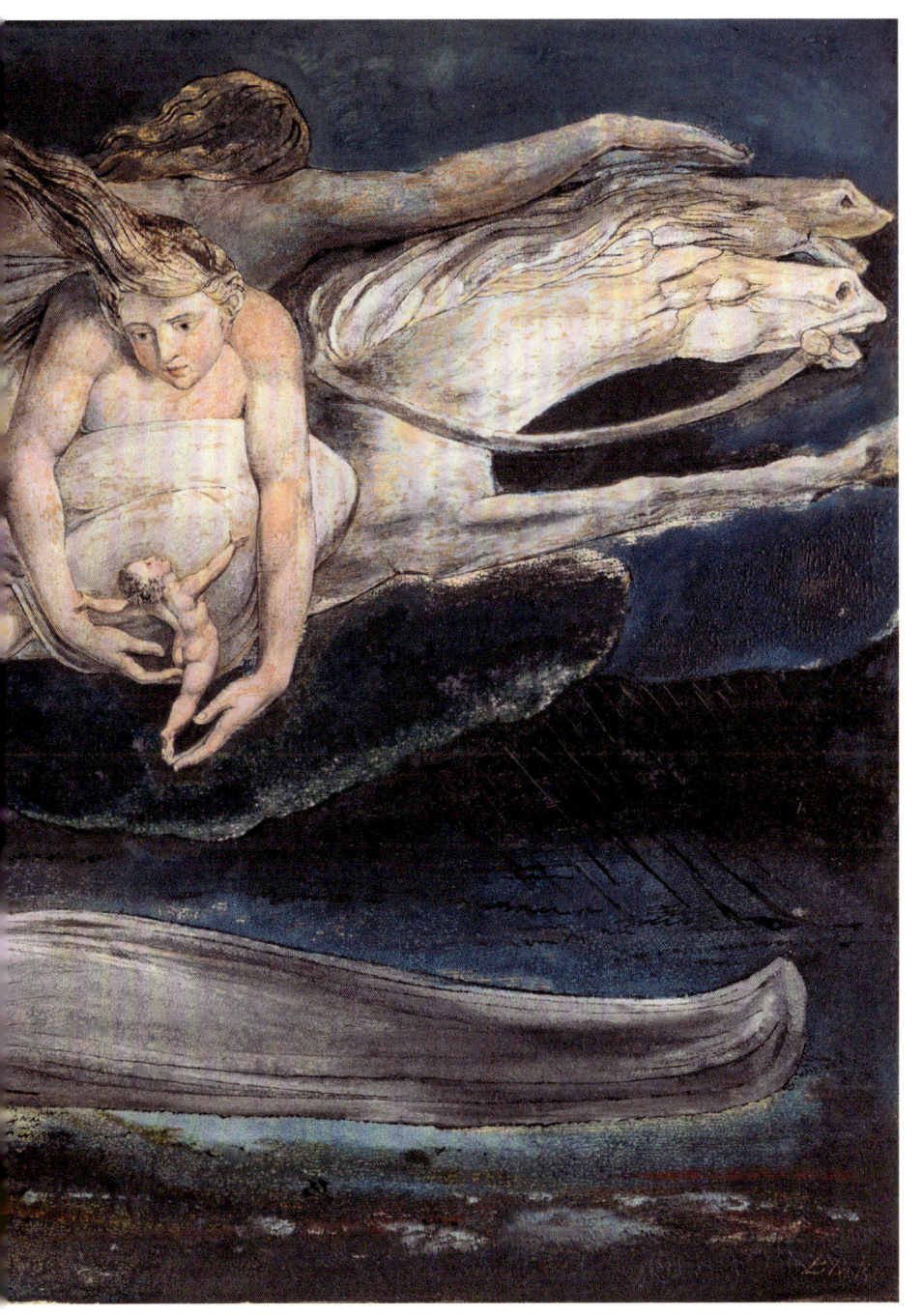

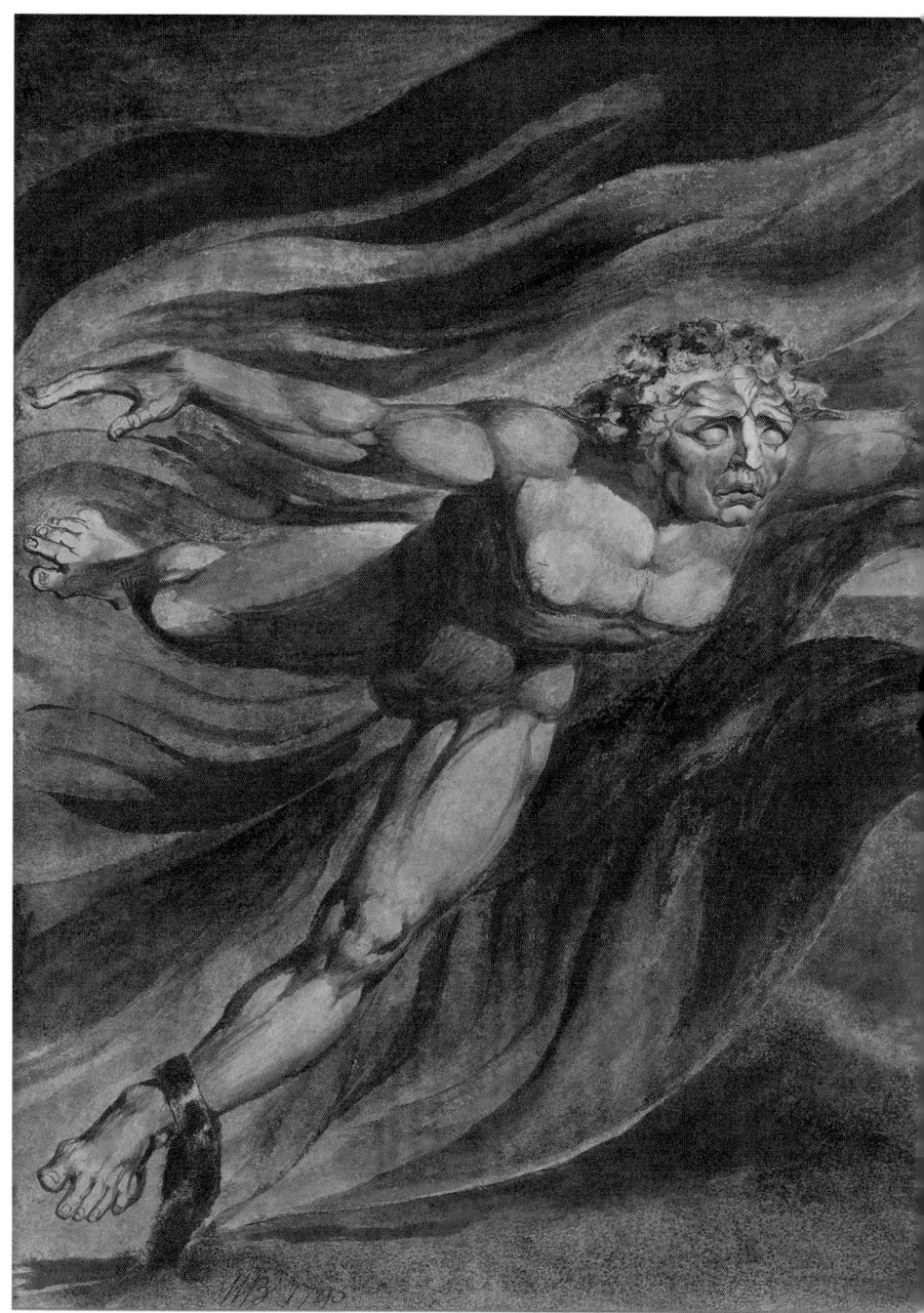

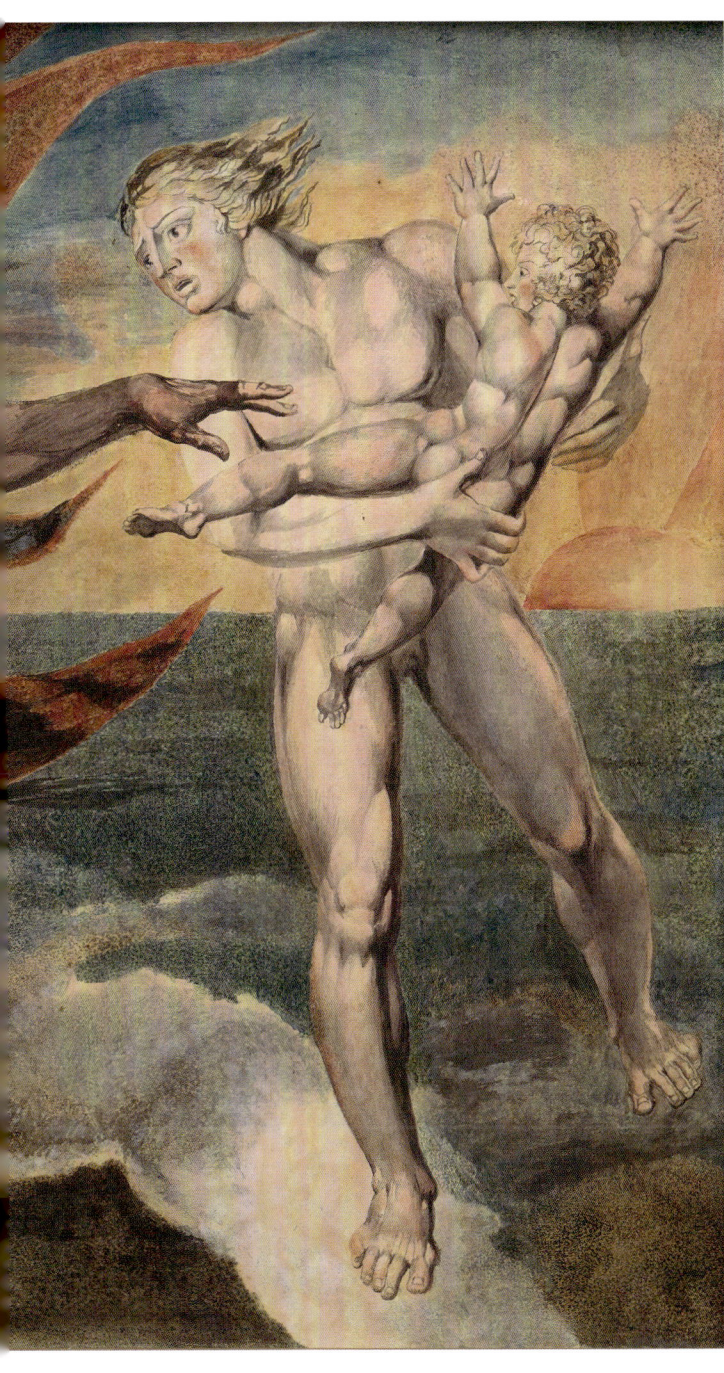

The Good and Evil Angels
1795–?c.1805
Colour print, ink and
watercolour on paper
44.5 × 59.4

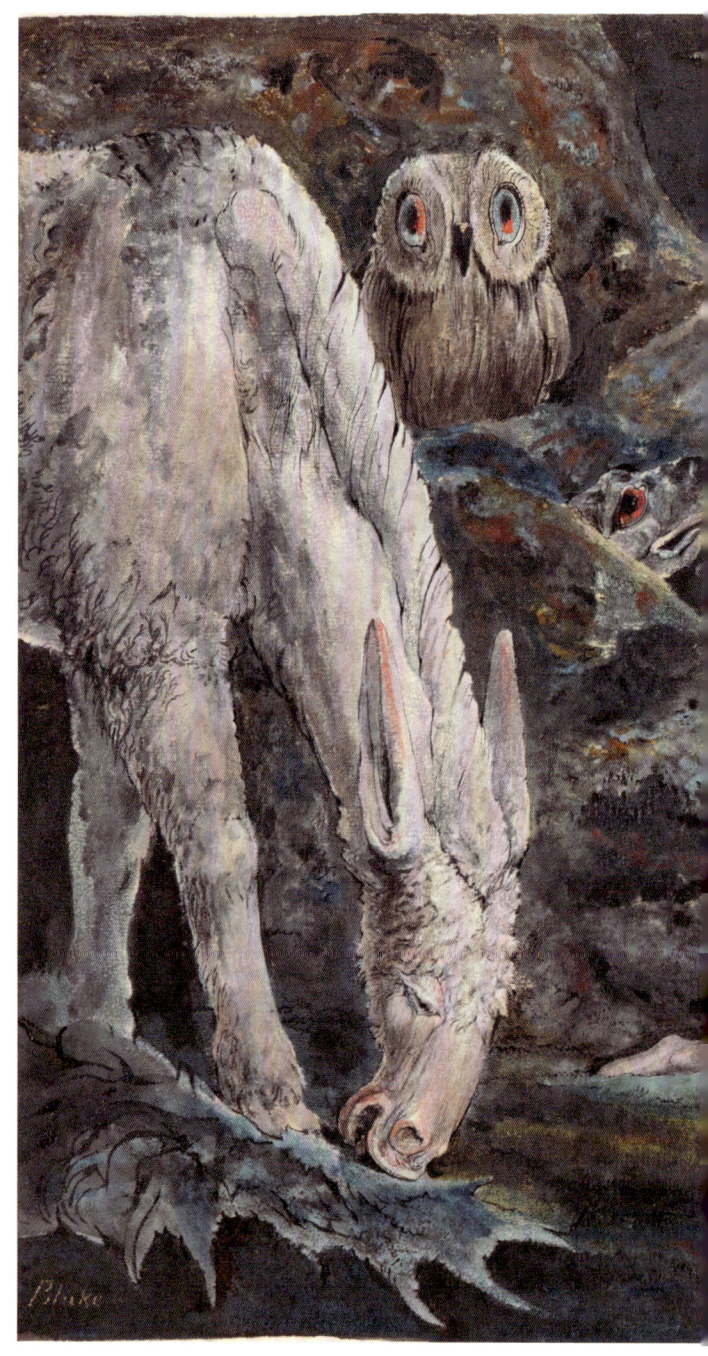

The Night of Enitharmon's Joy (formerly called 'Hecate')
c.1795
Colour print, ink, tempera
and watercolour on paper
43.9 × 58.1

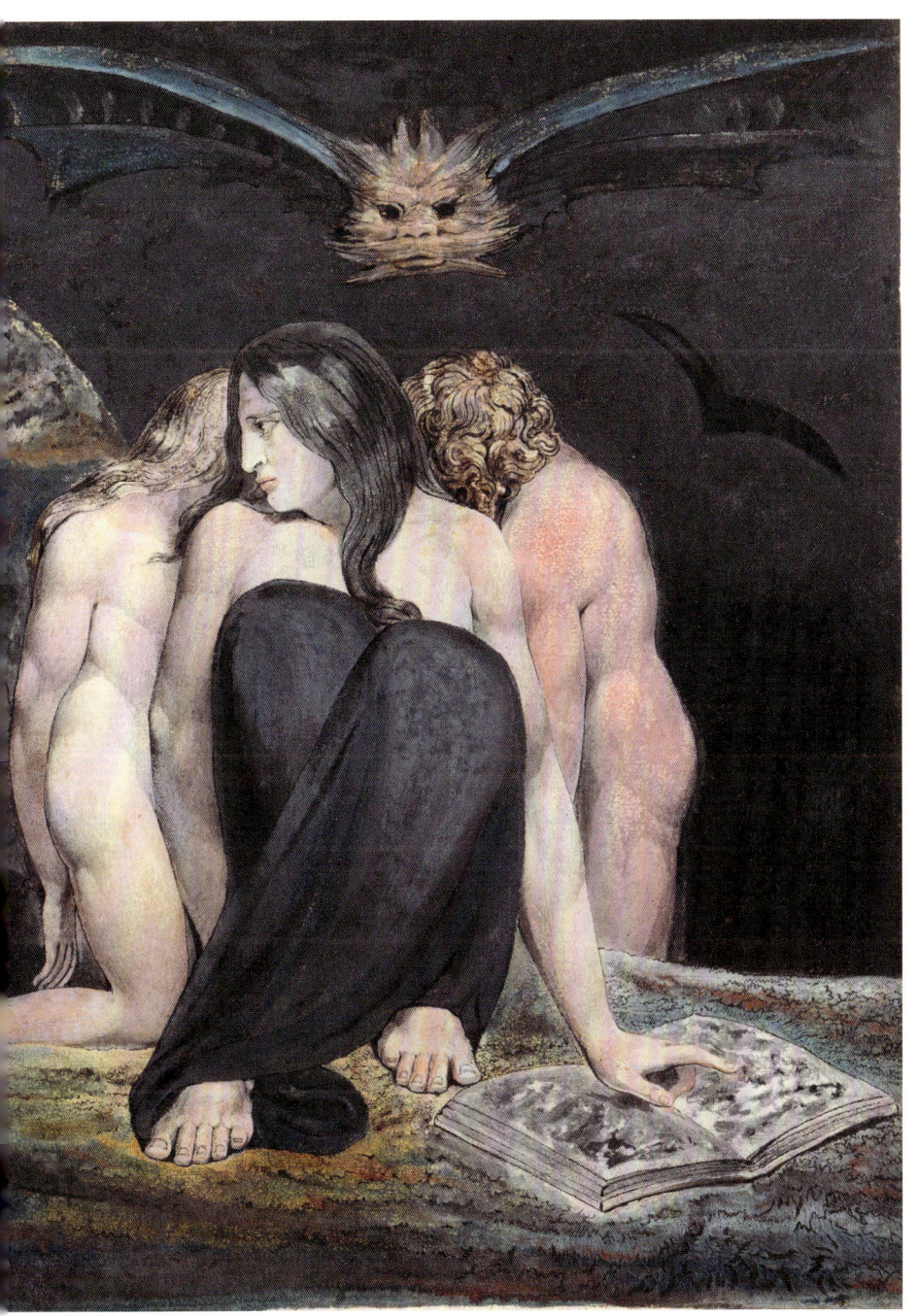

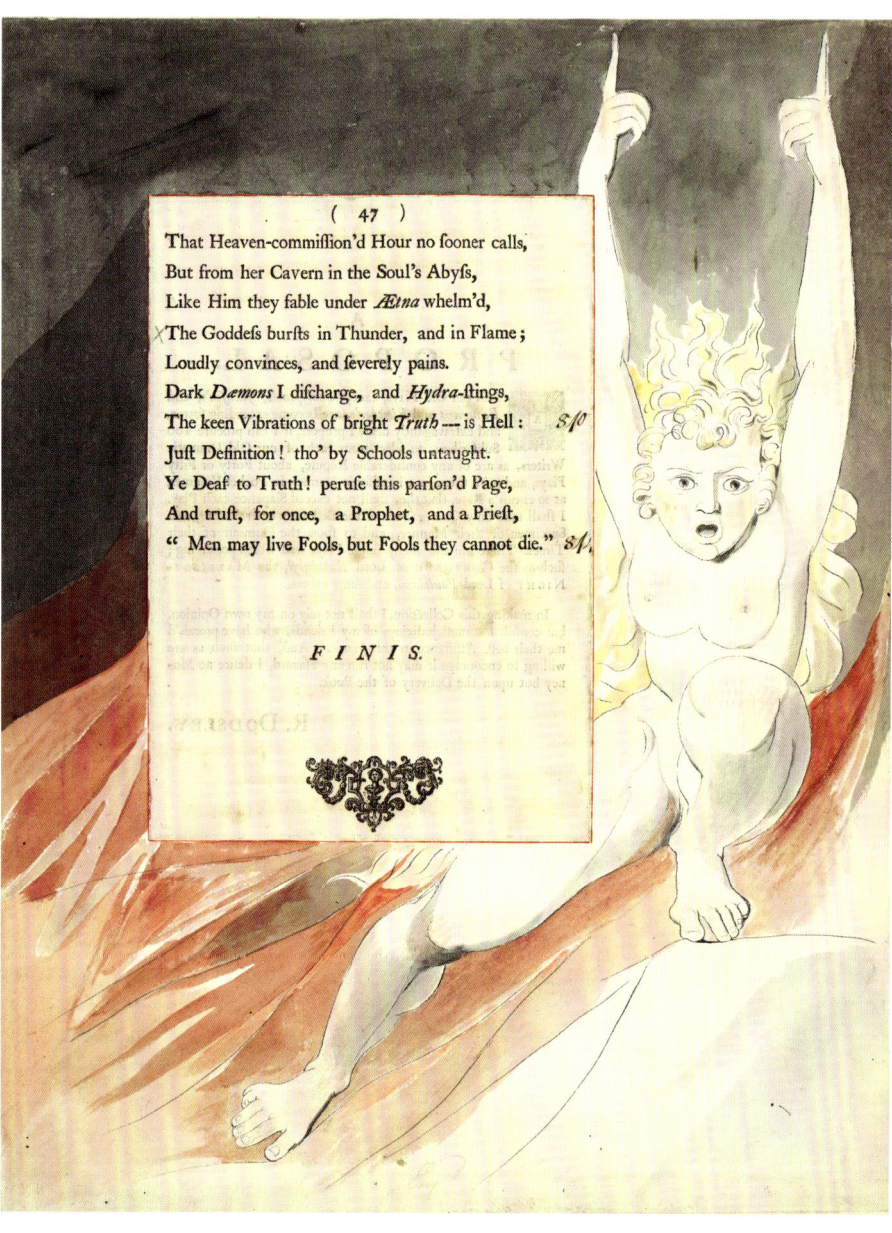

(47)

That Heaven-commiſſion'd Hour no ſooner calls,
But from her Cavern in the Soul's Abyſs,
Like Him they fable under *Ætna* whelm'd,
The Goddeſs burſts in Thunder, and in Flame;
Loudly convinces, and ſeverely pains.
Dark *Dæmons* I diſcharge, and *Hydra*-ſtings,
The keen Vibrations of bright *Truth* — is Hell:
Juſt Definition! tho' by Schools untaught.
Ye Deaf to Truth! peruſe this parſon'd Page,
And truſt, for once, a Prophet, and a Prieſt,
" Men may live Fools, but Fools they cannot die."

FINIS.

Night IV, page 47, 'That Heaven-commission'd Hour no sooner calls', illustration to Young's 'Night Thoughts' c.1795–7
Pen, ink and watercolour on paper
42 × 32.5

Night II, page 13, 'And seems to creep, decrepit with his Age', from Young's 'Night Thoughts' c.1795–7
Pen, ink, grey wash and watercolour over graphite on paper
42 × 32.5

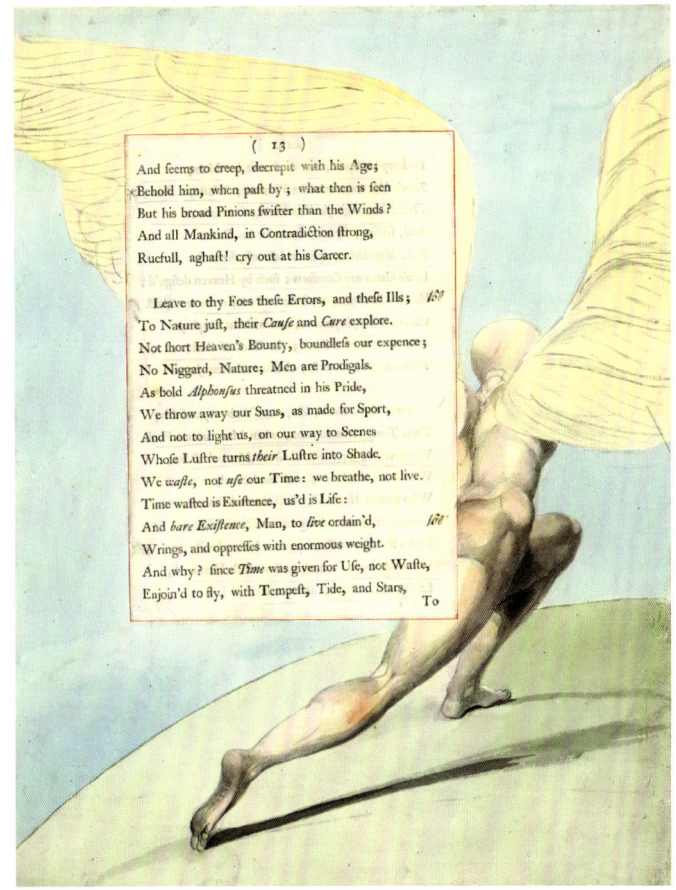

(13)

And seems to creep, decrepit with his Age;
Behold him, when past by; what then is seen
But his broad Pinions swifter than the Winds?
And all Mankind, in Contradiction strong,
Ruefull, aghast! cry out at his Career.

Leave to thy Foes these Errors, and these Ills; 150
To Nature just, their *Cause* and *Cure* explore.
Not short Heaven's Bounty, boundless our expence;
No Niggard, Nature; Men are Prodigals.
As bold *Alphonsus* threatned in his Pride,
We throw away our Suns, as made for Sport,
And not to light us, on our way to Scenes
Whose Lustre turns *their* Lustre into Shade.
We *waste*, not *use* our Time: we breathe, not live.
Time wasted is Existence, us'd is Life:
And *bare Existence*, Man, to *live* ordain'd, 160
Wrings, and oppresses with enormous weight.
And why? since *Time* was given for Use, not Waste,
Enjoin'd to fly, with Tempest, Tide, and Stars,
To

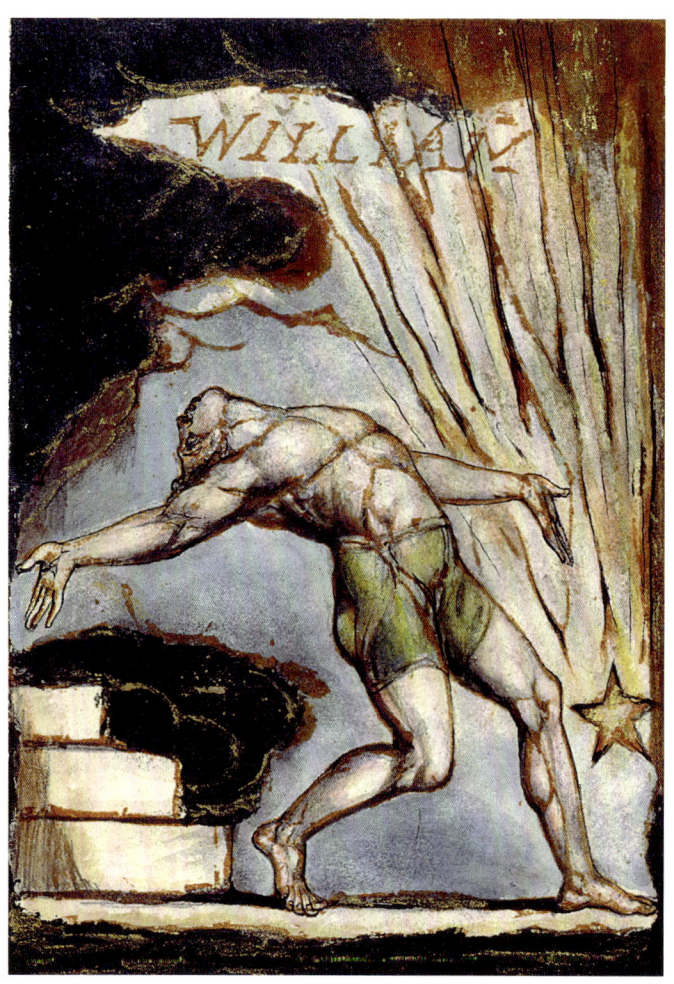

'Milton a Poem' plate 32
(Copy D) composed
c.1804–11, printed 1818
Relief etching with hand-
colouring on paper
Plates range between
13.5 × 9.6 and 16.9 × 12

David Delivered out of Many
Waters c.1805
Ink and watercolour
on paper
41.5 × 34.8

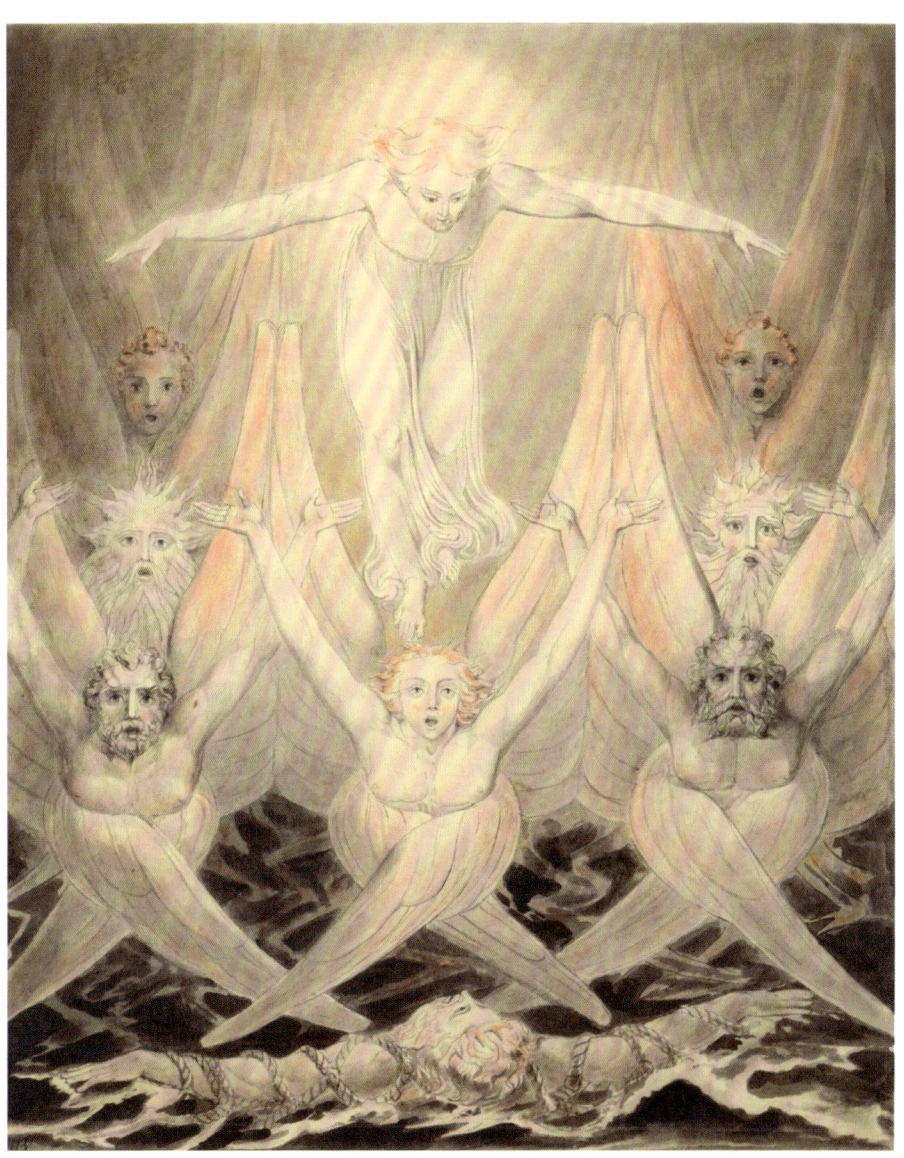

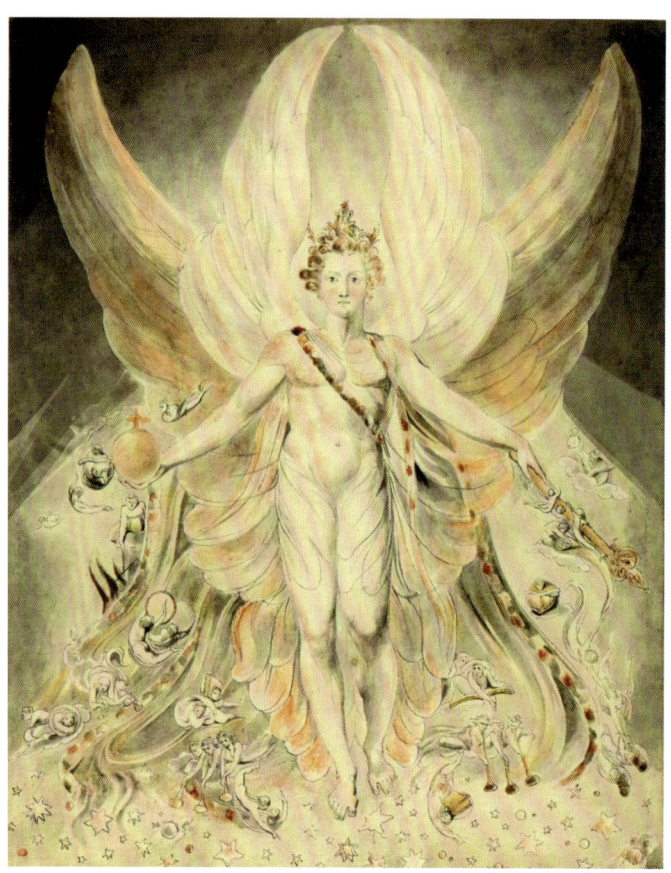

Satan in his Original Glory:
'Thou wast Perfect till Iniquity
was Found in Thee' c.1805
Ink and watercolour on paper
42.9 × 33.9

Satan Watching the Endearments
of Adam and Eve 1808
Pen, ink and watercolour
on paper
25.7 × 21.8

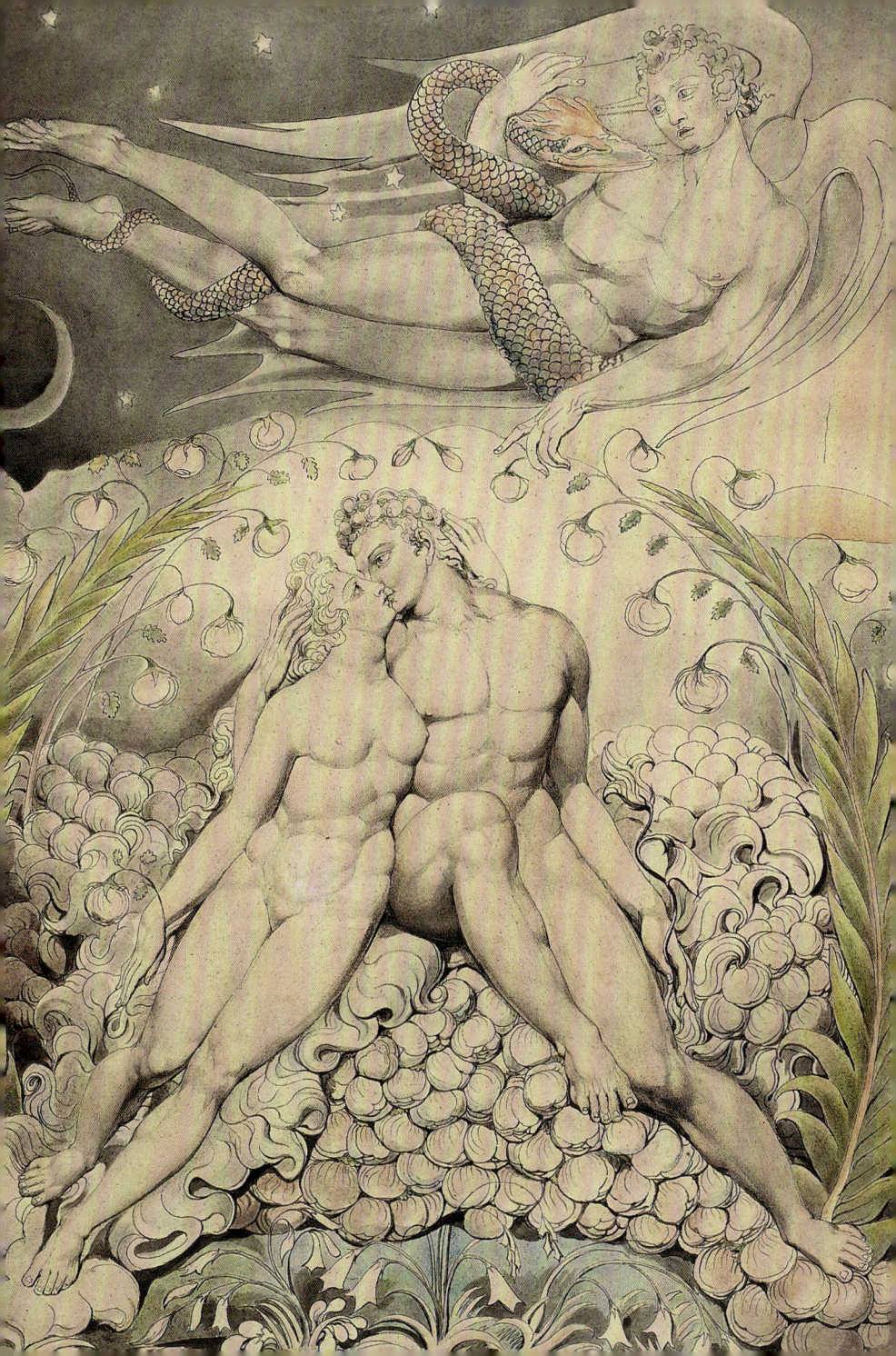

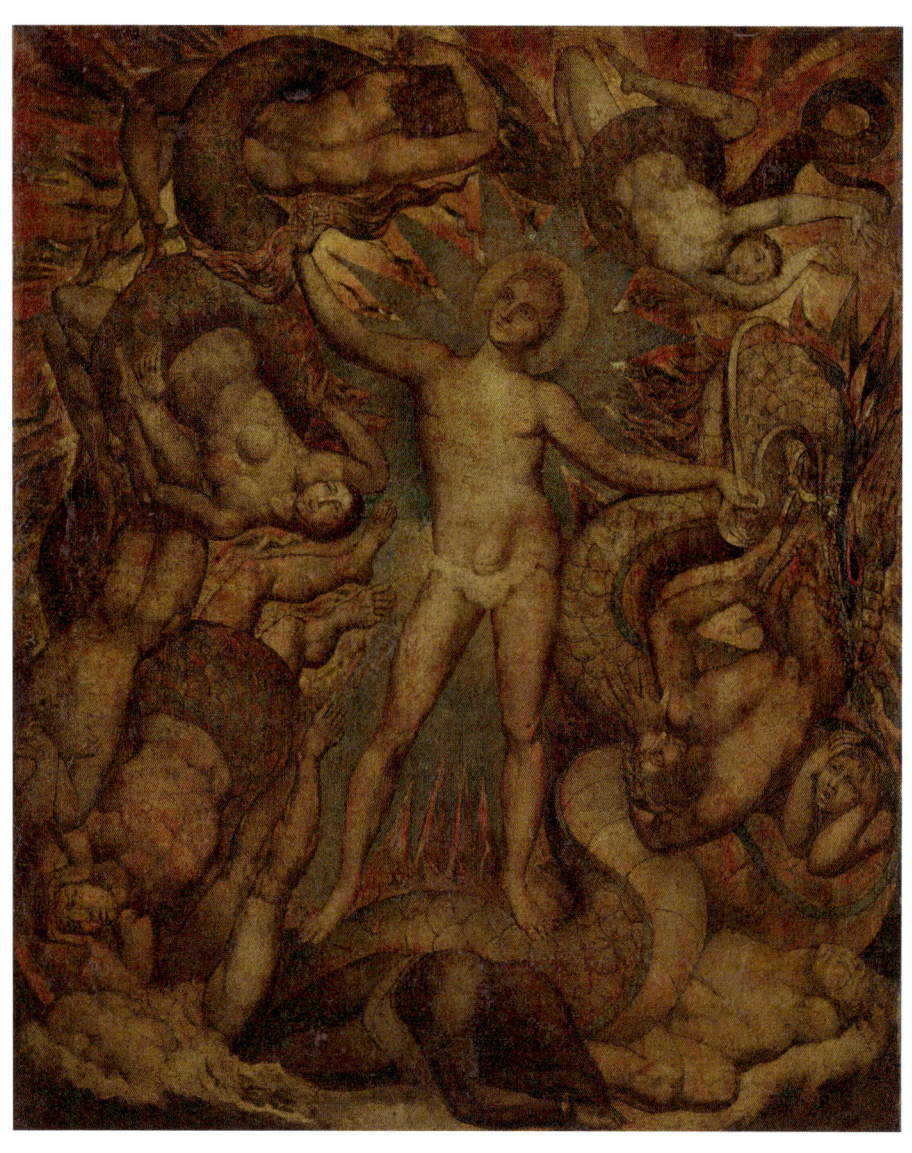

The Spiritual Form of Nelson
Guiding Leviathan c.1805–9
Tempera on canvas
76.2 × 62.5

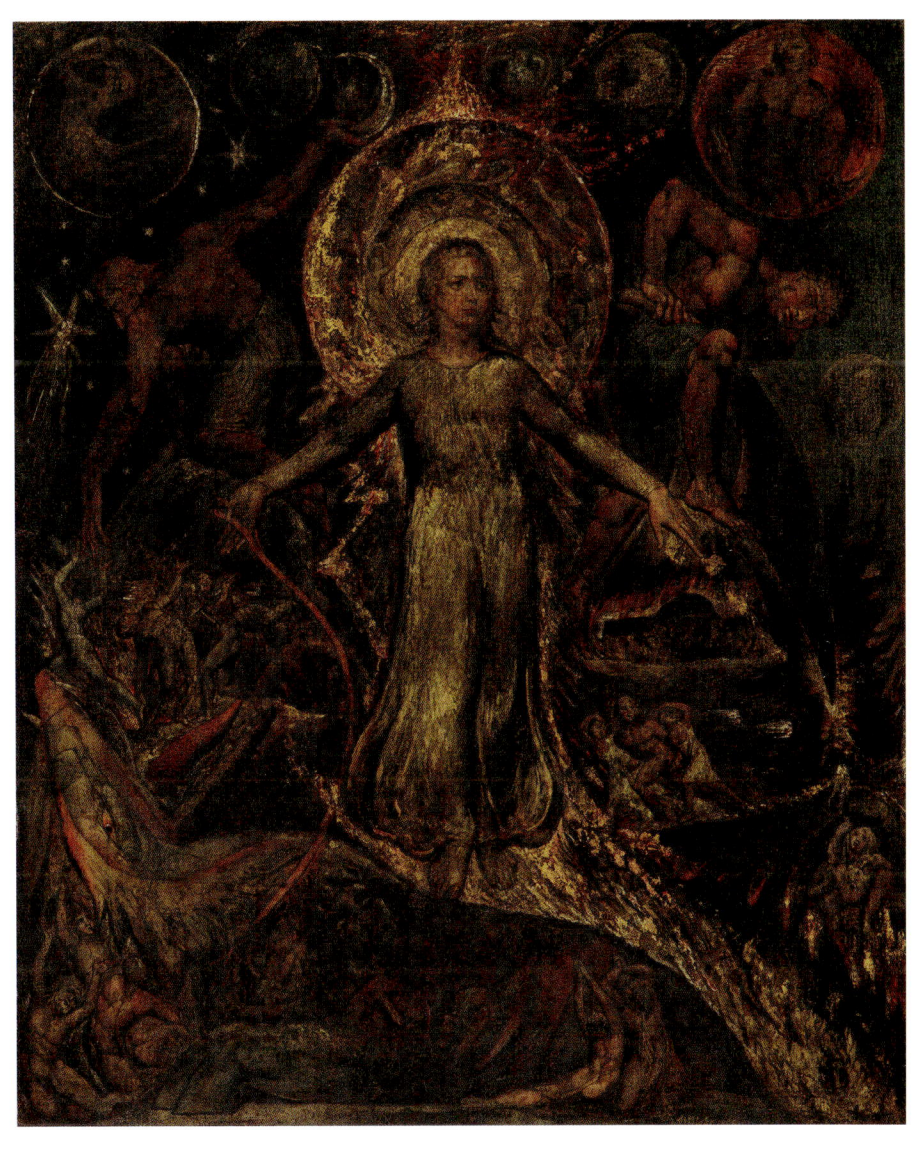

The Spiritual Form of Pitt
Guiding Behemoth c.1805
Tempera on paper
74 × 62.7

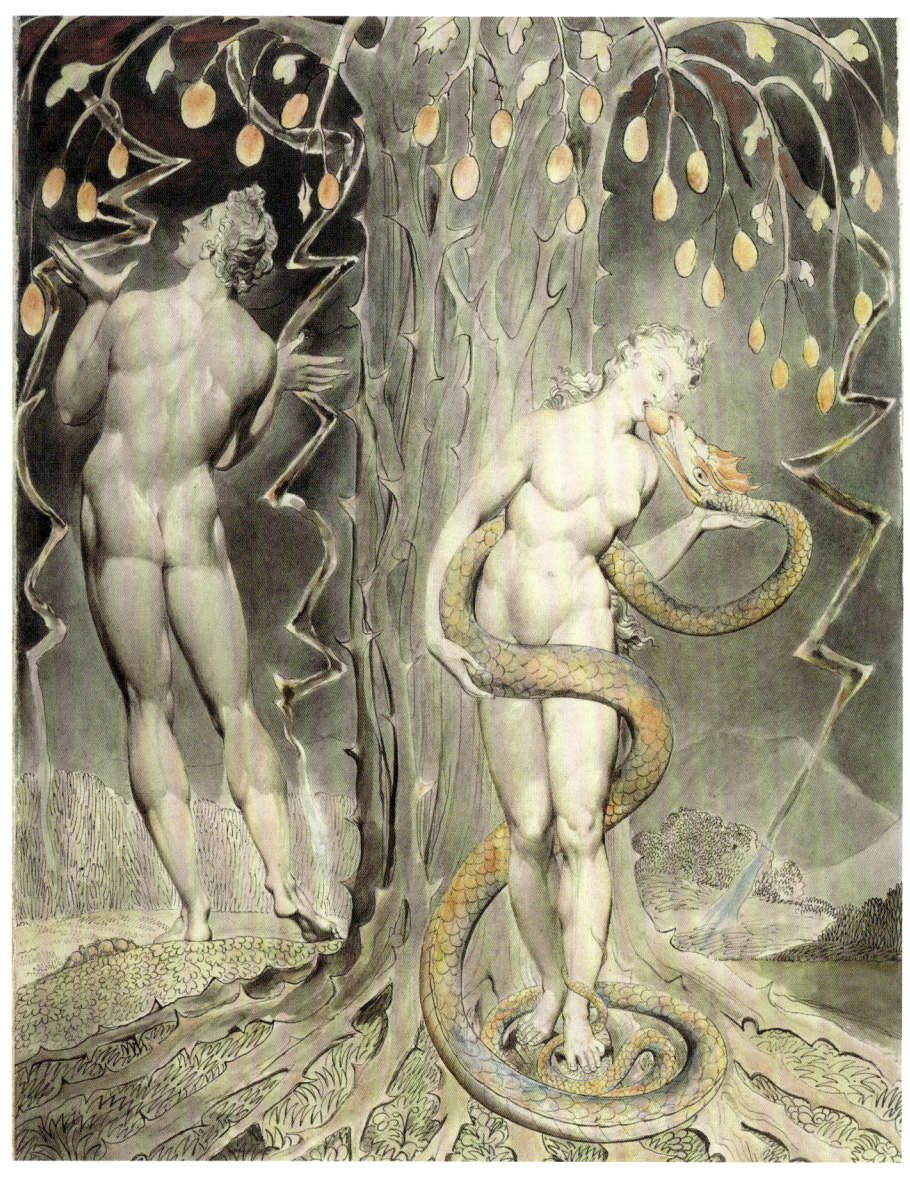

The Temptation and Fall of Eve
1808
Pen, ink and watercolour
on paper
49.7 × 38.7

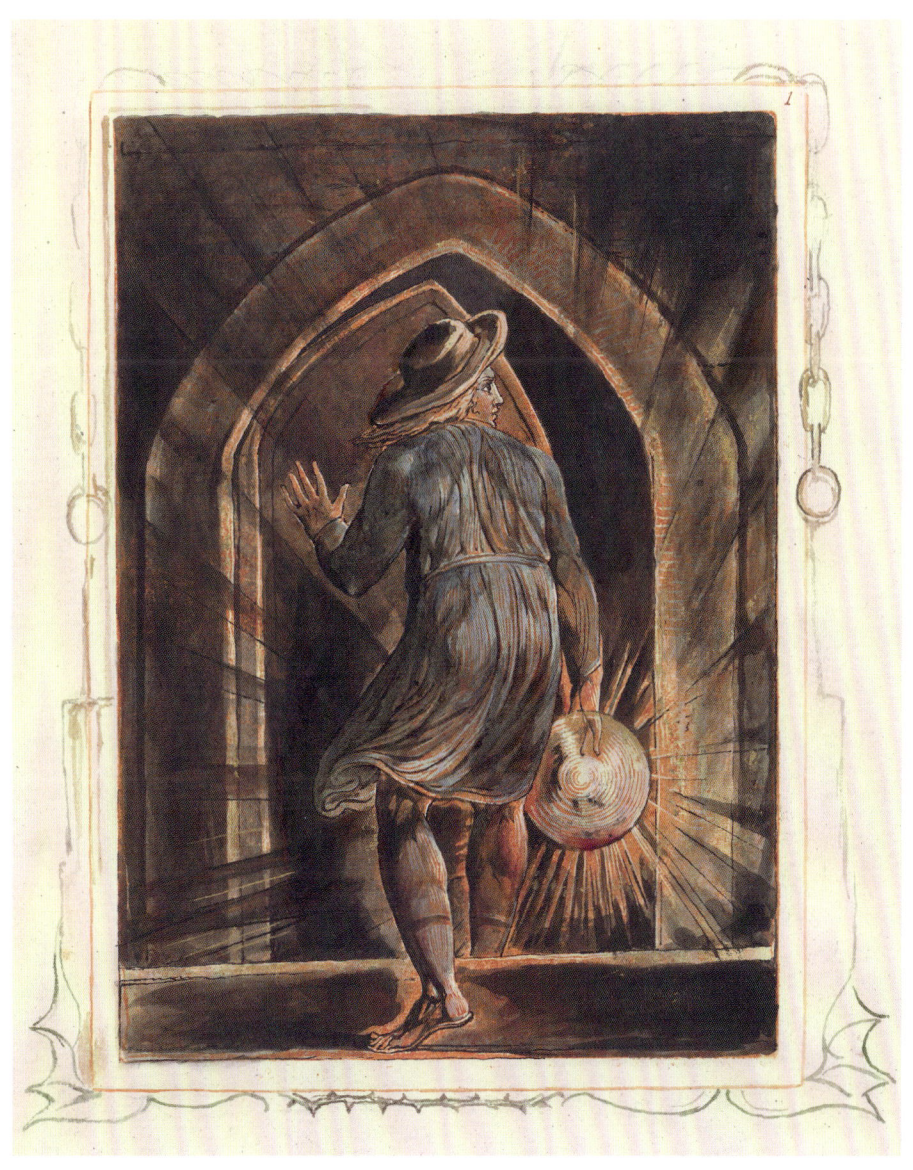

'Jerusalem' plate 1 composed
c.1804–20, printed c.1821
Relief etching with hand-
colouring on paper
Plate sizes range between
22.7 × 17.1 and 20.1 × 14

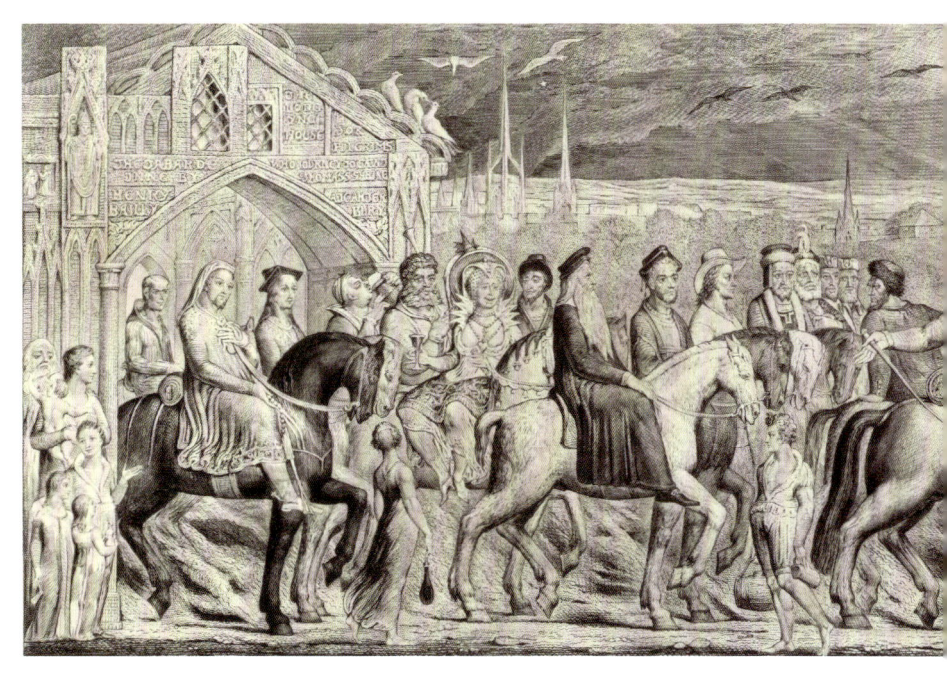

Chaucer's Canterbury Pilgrims
1810, reprinted before 1881
Engraving on paper
35.7 × 96.7

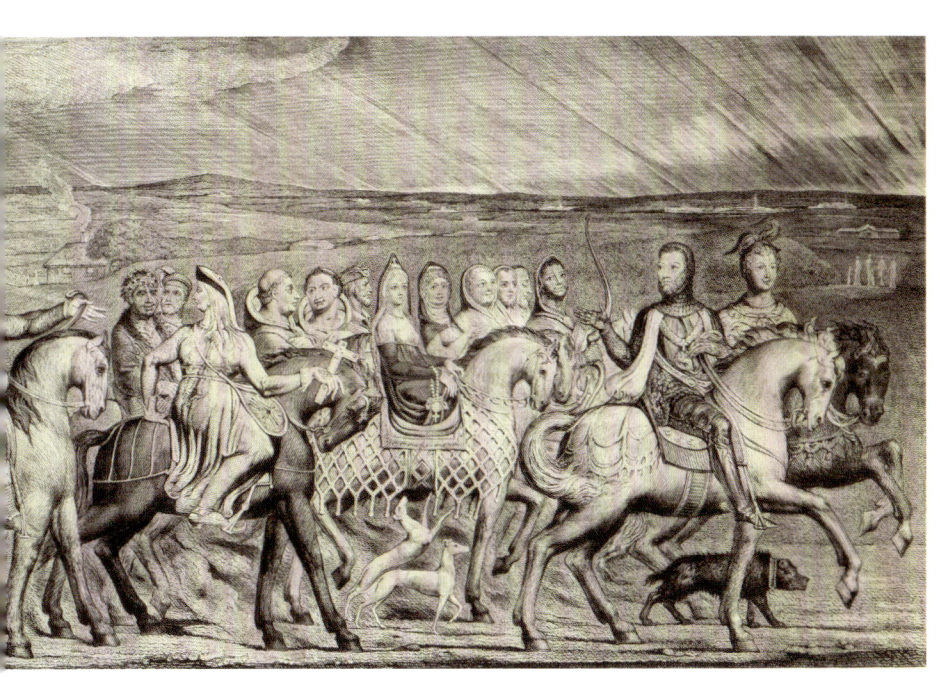

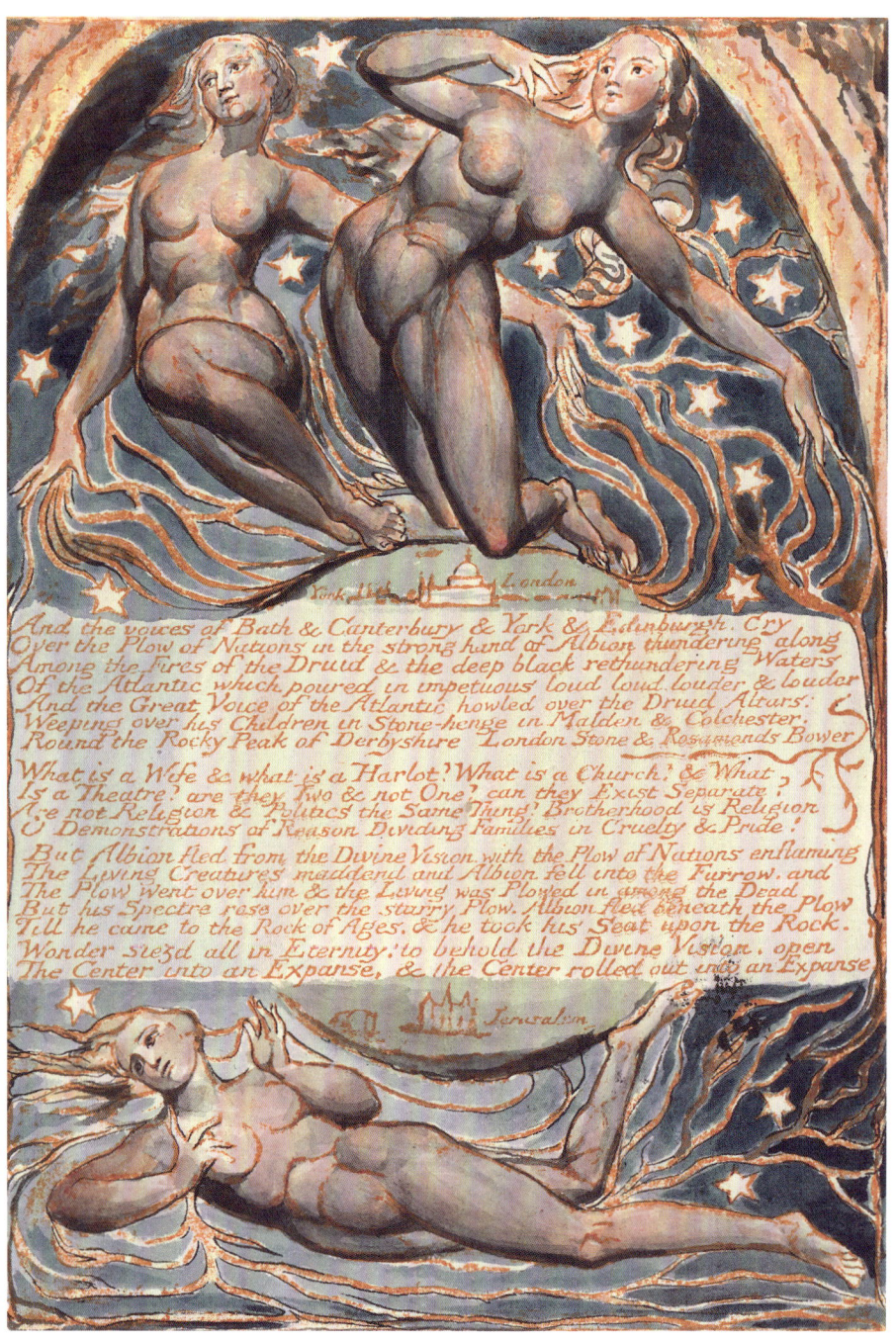

And the voices of Bath & Canterbury & York & Edinburgh, Cry
Over the Plow of Nations in the strong hand of Albion thundering along
Among the fires of the Druid & the deep black rethundering Waters
Of the Atlantic which poured in impetuous loud loud, louder, & louder,
And the Great Voice of the Atlantic howled over the Druid Altars,
Weeping over his Children in Stone-henge in Malden & Colchester.
Round the Rocky Peak of Derbyshire London Stone & Rosamonds Bower

What is a Wife & what is a Harlot? What is a Church? & What
Is a Theatre? are they Two & not One? can they Exist Separate?
Are not Religion & Politics the Same Thing? Brotherhood is Religion
O Demonstrations of Reason Dividing Families in Cruelty & Pride!

But Albion fled from the Divine Vision, with the Plow of Nations enflaming
The Living Creatures maddend and Albion fell into the Furrow. and
The Plow went over him & the Living was Plowed in among the Dead,
But his Spectre rose over the starry Plow. Albion fled beneath the Plow
Till he came to the Rock of Ages. & he took his Seat upon the Rock.
Wonder siezd all in Eternity! to behold the Divine Vision. open
The Center into an Expanse, & the Center rolled out into an Expanse

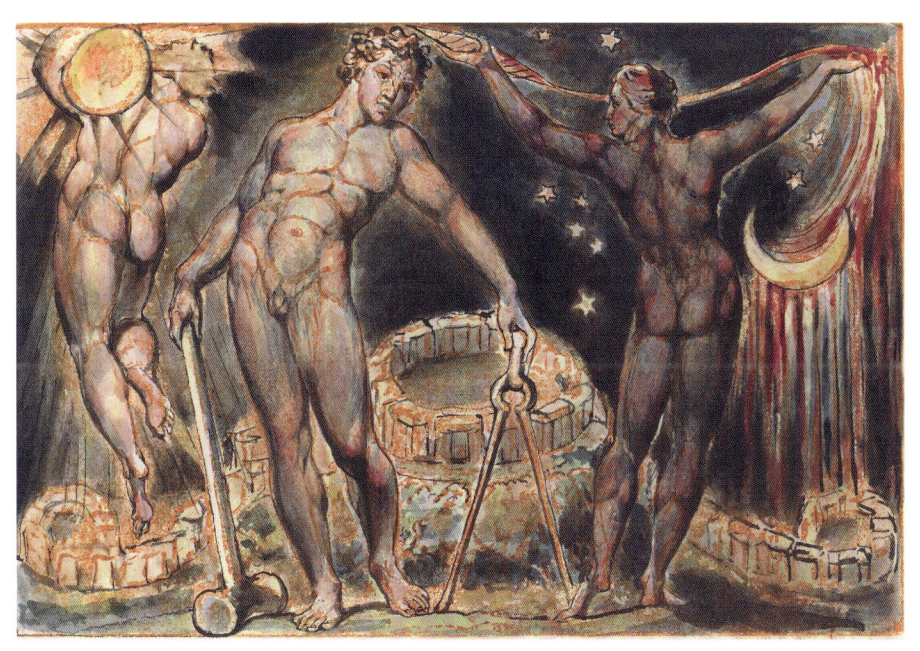

'Jerusalem' plate 57
composed c.1804–20,
printed c.1821
Relief etching with hand-
colouring on paper
Plate sizes range between
22.7 × 17.1 and 20.1 × 14

'Jerusalem' plate 100
composed c.1804–20,
printed c.1821
Relief etching with hand-
colouring on paper
Plate sizes range between
22.7 × 17.1 and 20.1 × 14

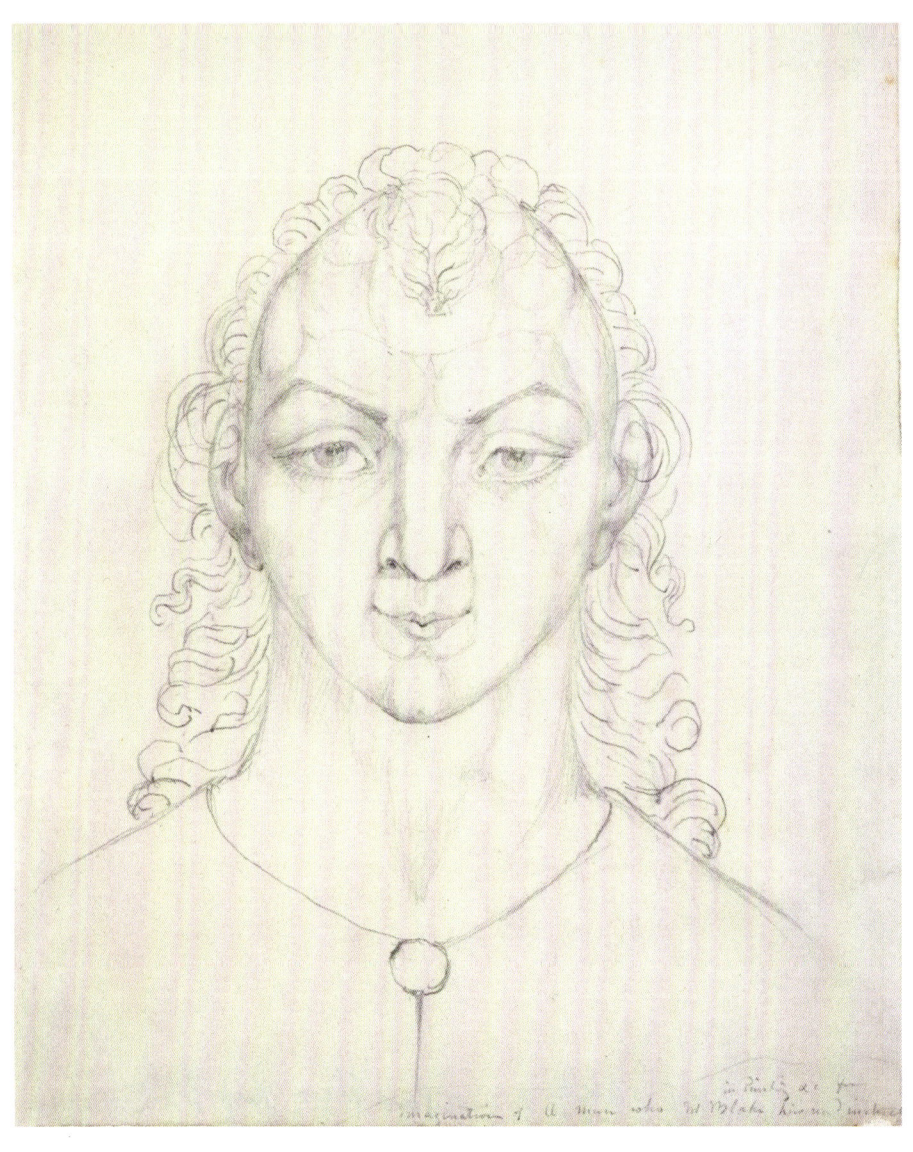

after William Blake
The Man Who Taught Blake
Painting in his Dreams
(counterproof) after c.1819–20
Graphite on paper
29.6 × 23.5

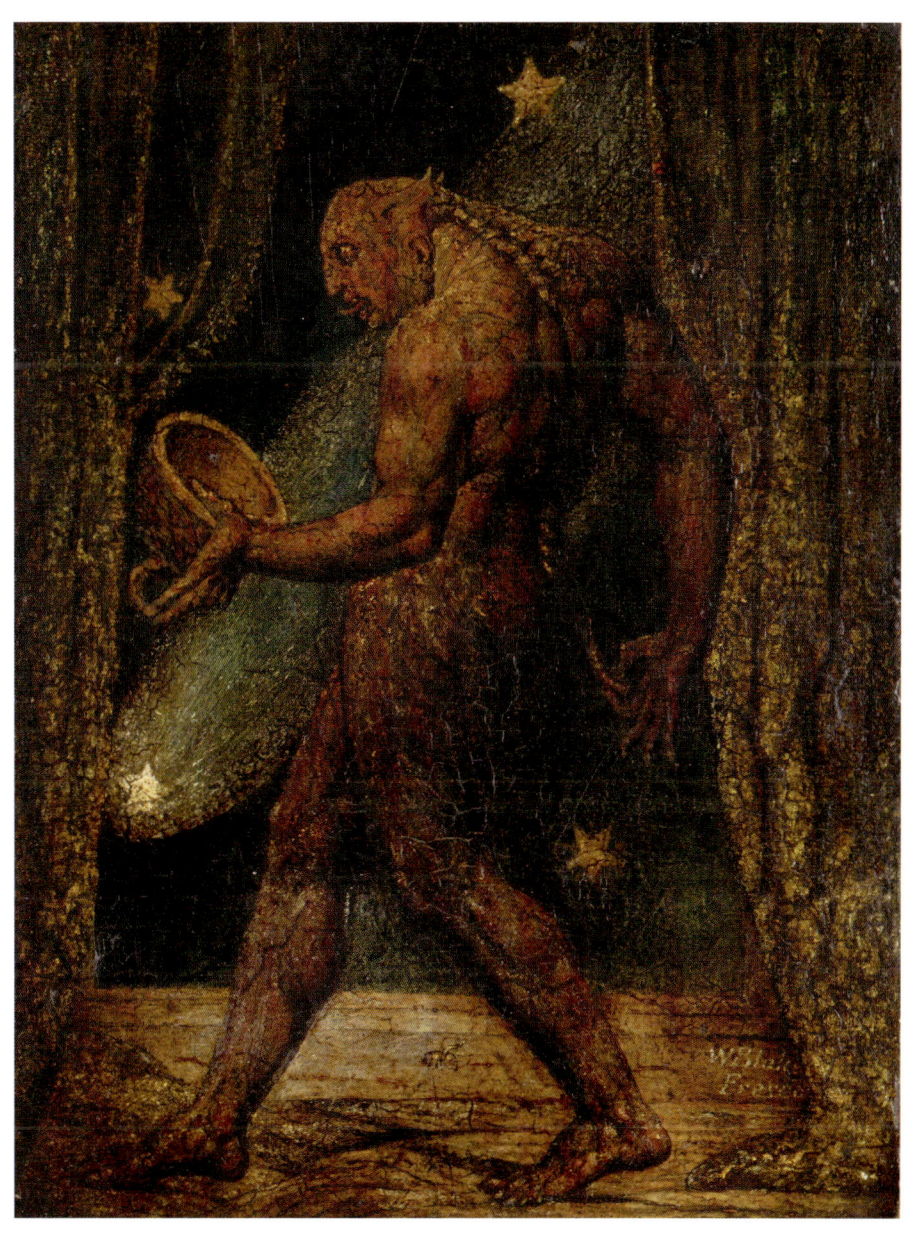

The Ghost of a Flea c.1819–20
Tempera and gold on
mahogany
21.4 × 16.2

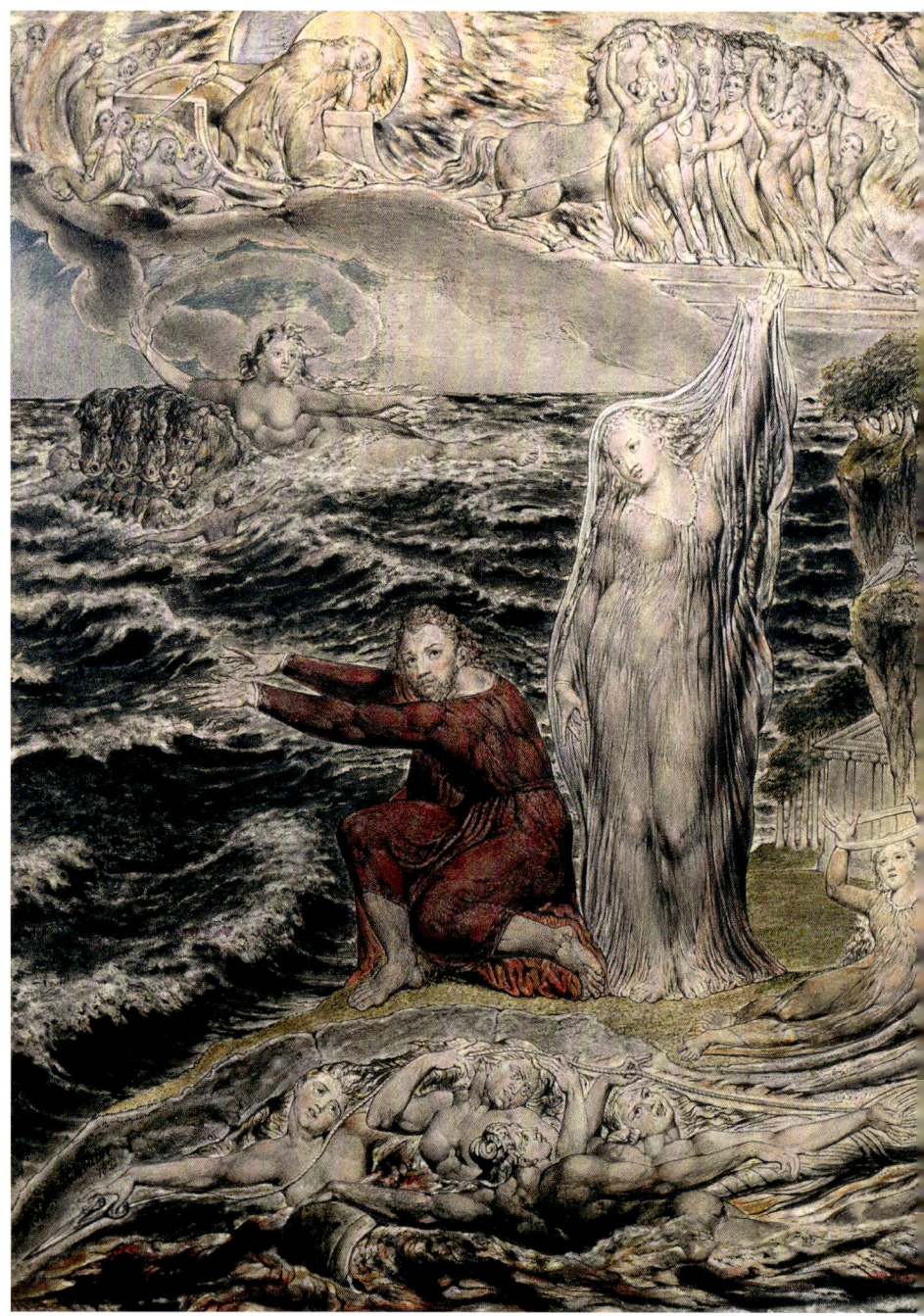

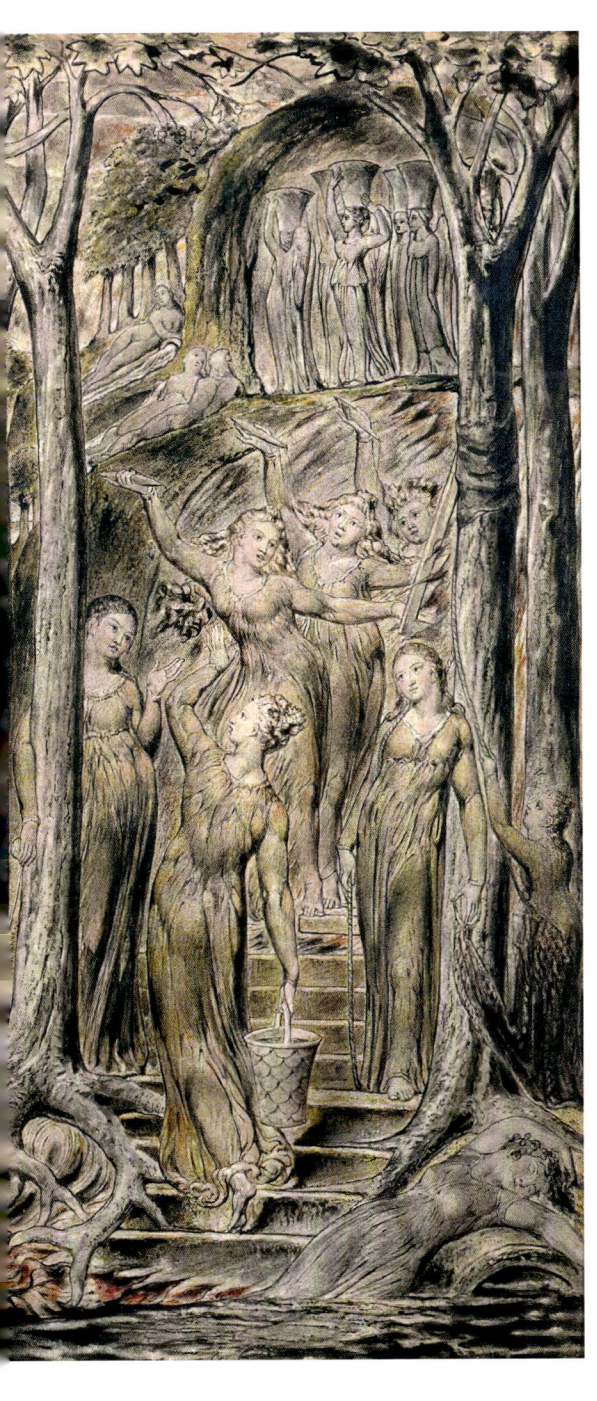

The Sea of Time and Space 1821
Pen, ink, watercolour,
gouache and gesso on paper
47.8 × 57.4

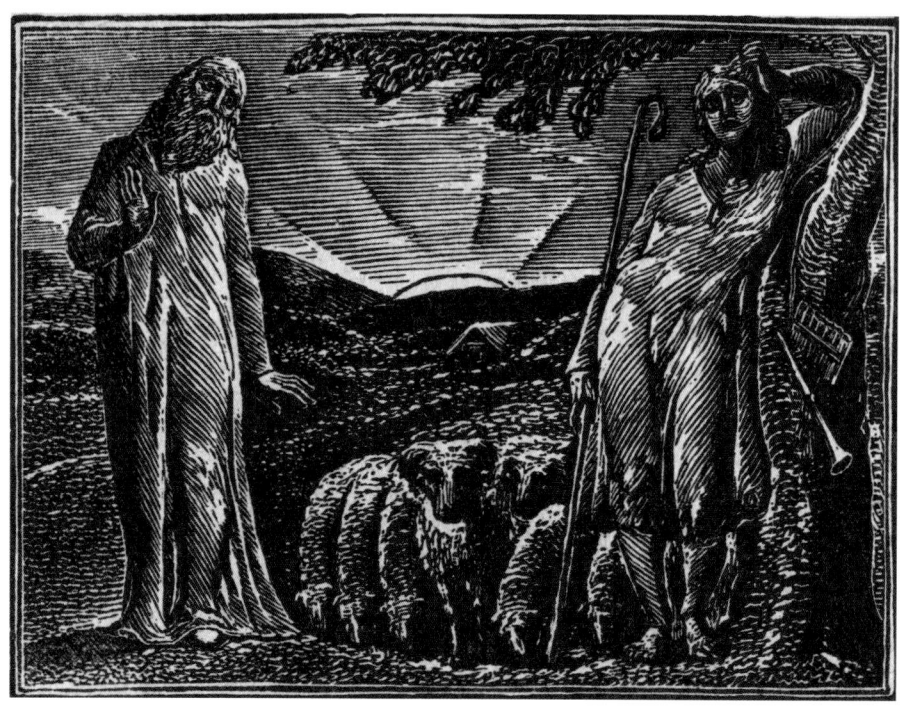

after William Blake
*Frontispiece: 'Thenot and
Colinet'* c.1821, printed 1830
Wood engraving on paper
6.2 × 8.4

Edward Calvert
The Return Home 1830
Wood engraving on paper
4.1 × 7.6

OVERLEAF
*Dante Running from the Three
Beasts* 1824–7
Pen, ink and watercolour
over graphite and black
chalk on paper
37.3 × 52.8

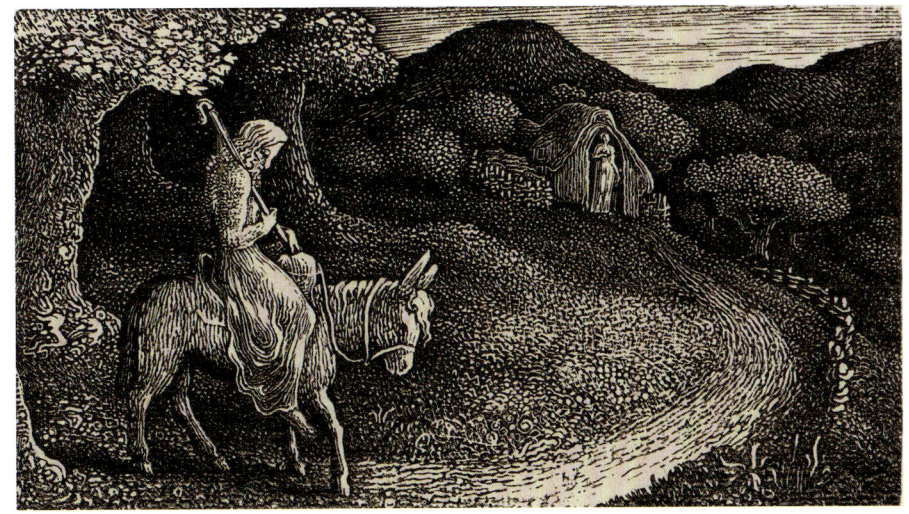

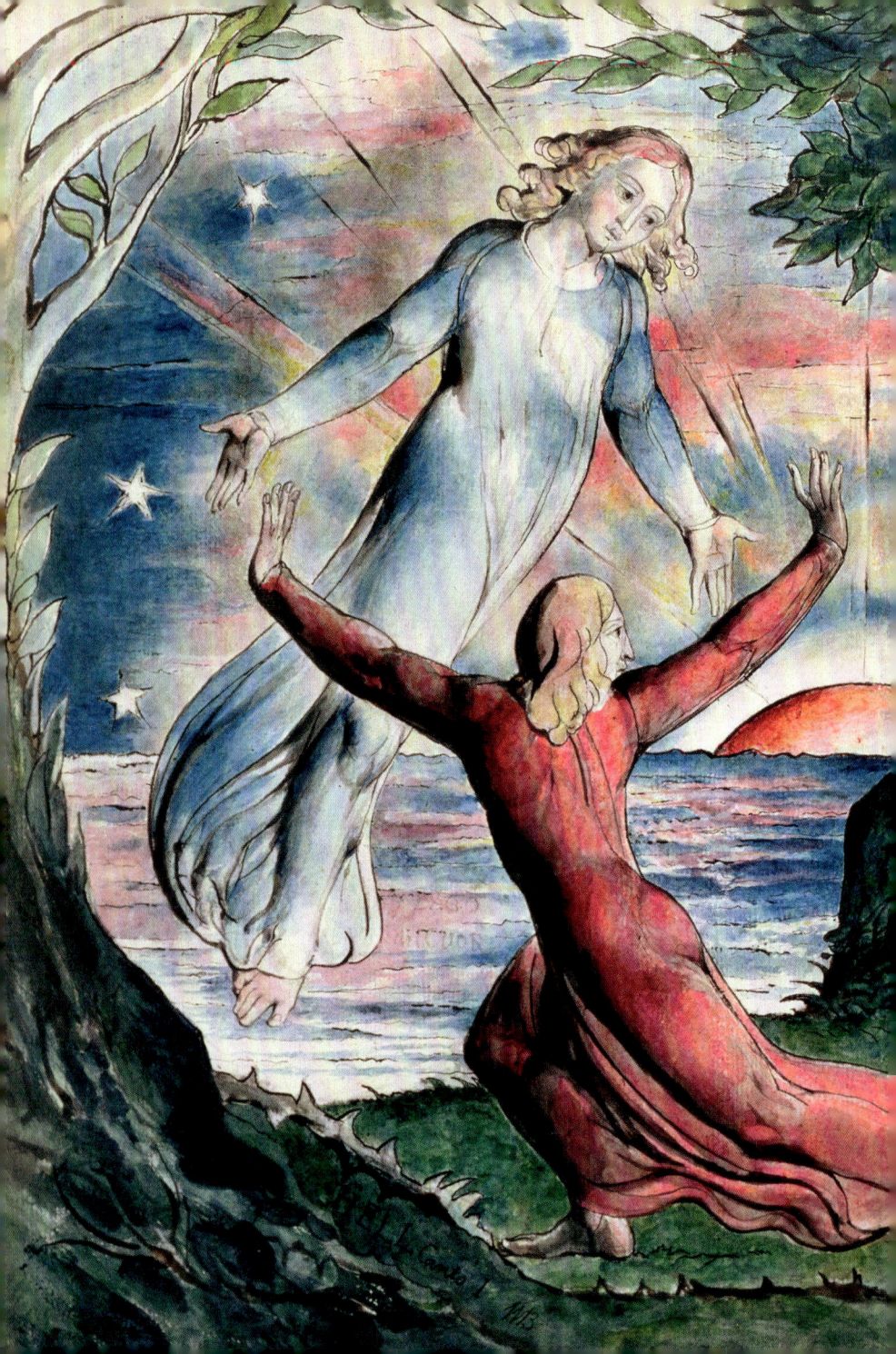

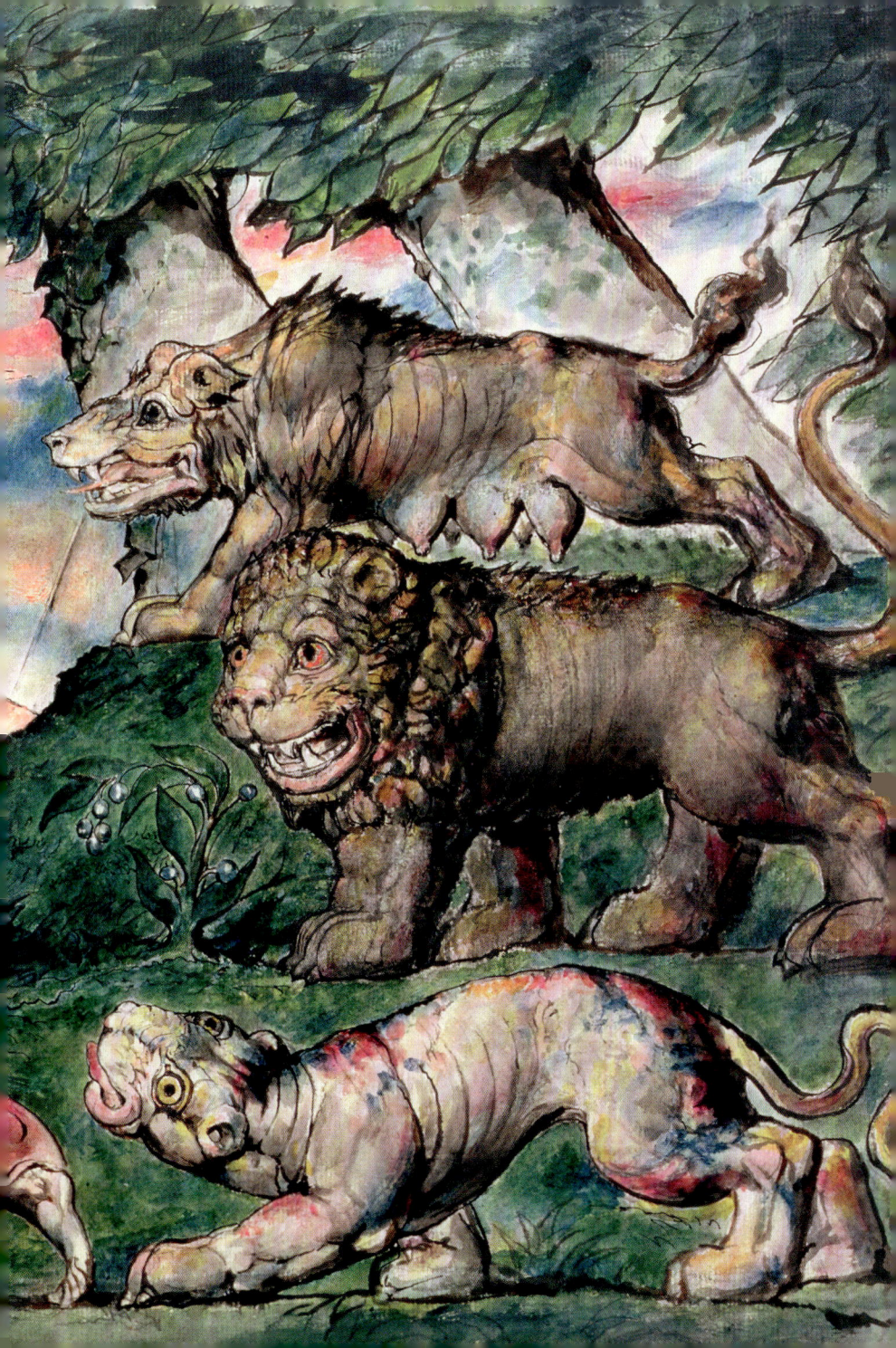

after William Blake
Colinet's 'Fond Desire Strange Lands to Know' c.1821,
printed 1830
Wood engraving on paper
3.7 × 7.4

The Inscription over the Gate
1824–7
Graphite, ink and
watercolour on paper
52.7 × 37.4

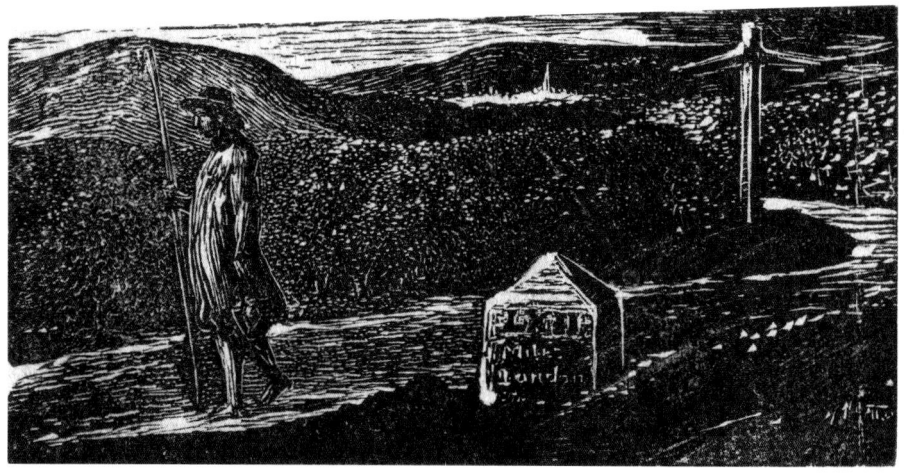

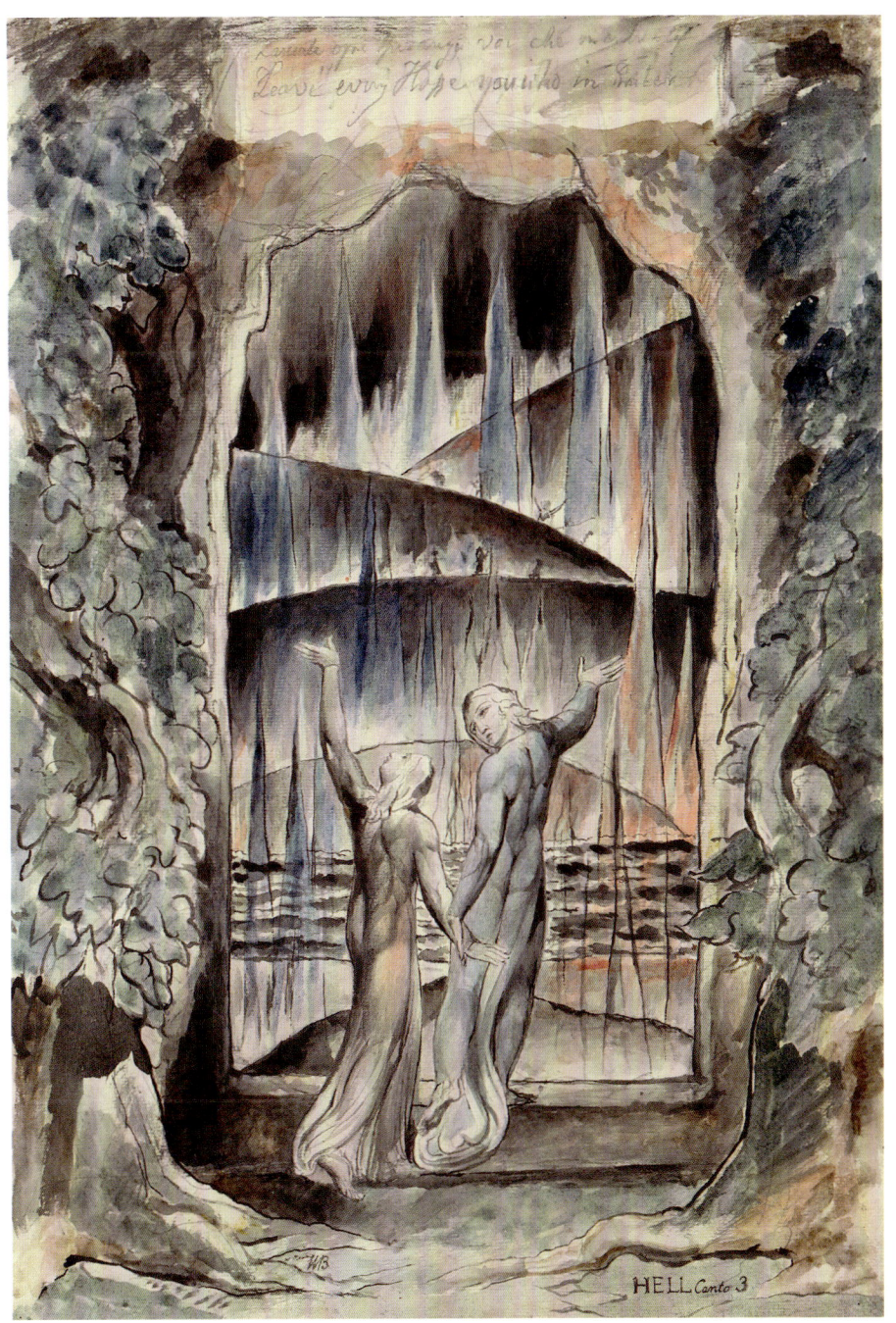

HELL Canto 3

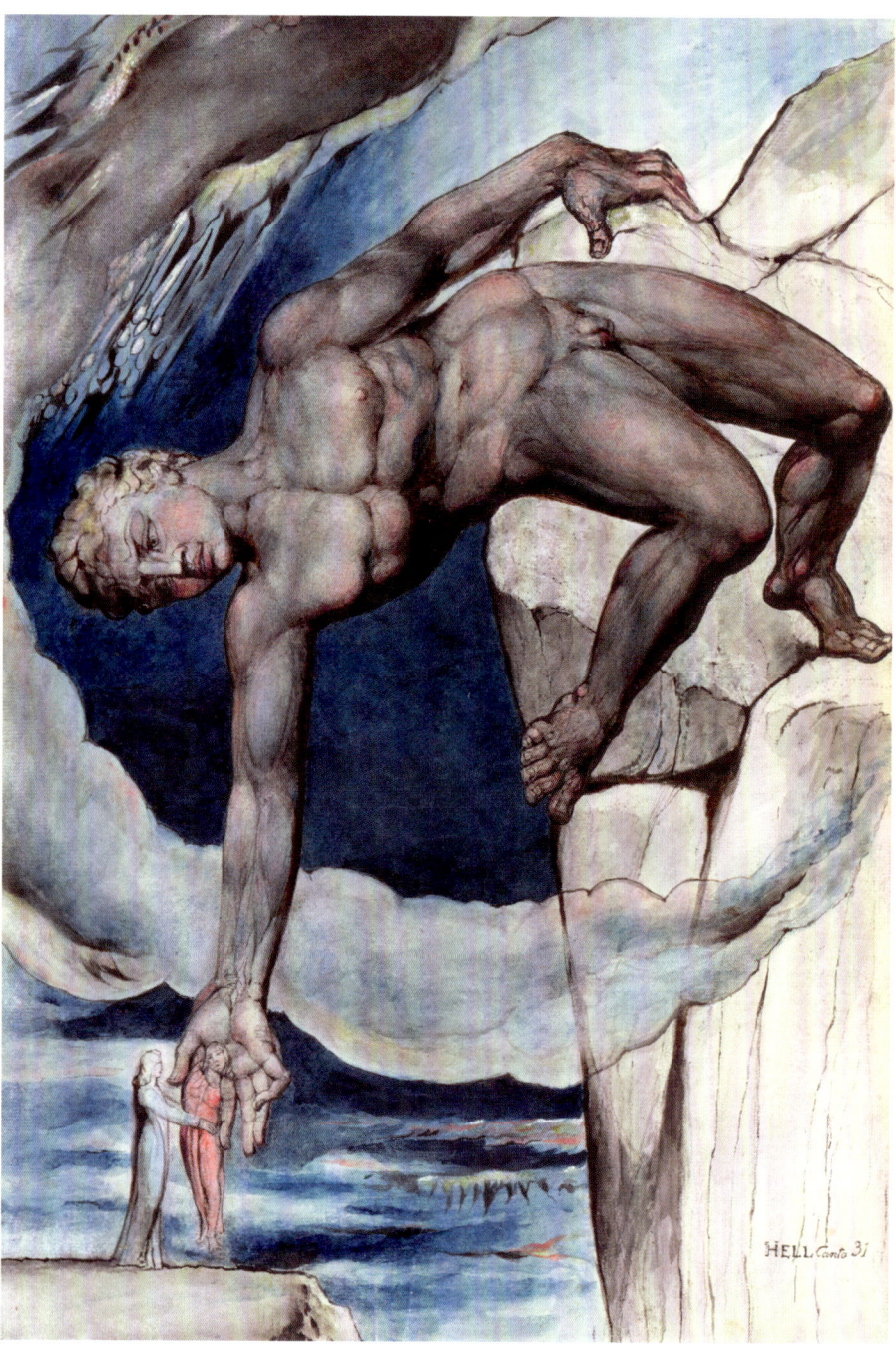

HELL Canto 31

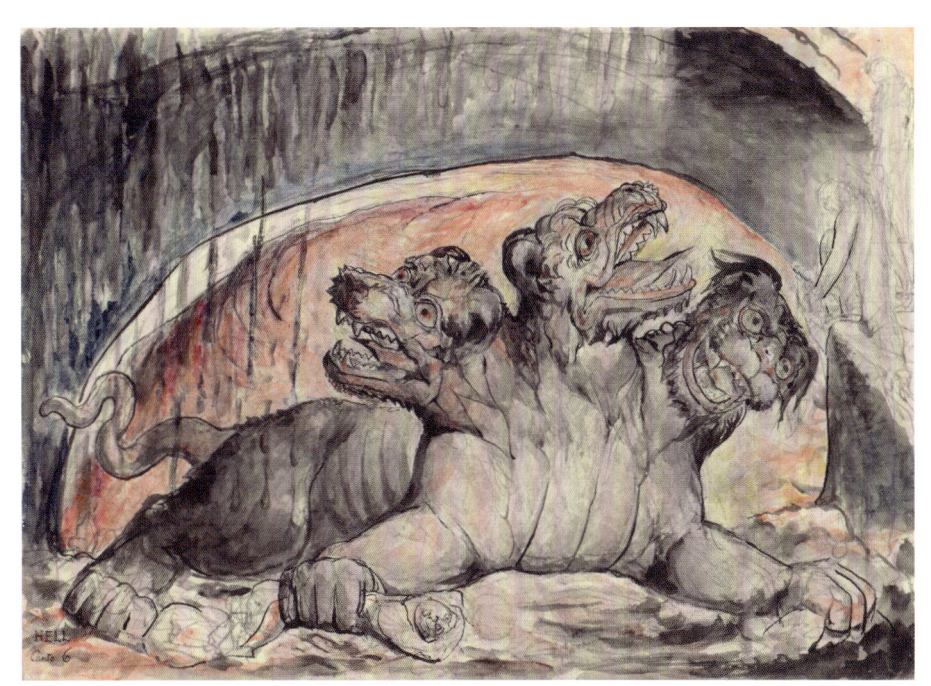

*Antaeus Setting Down Dante
and Virgil in the Last Circle
of Hell* 1824–7
Pen and watercolour on
paper
52.6 × 37.4

Cerberus 1824–7
Graphite, ink and
watercolour on paper
37.2 × 52.8

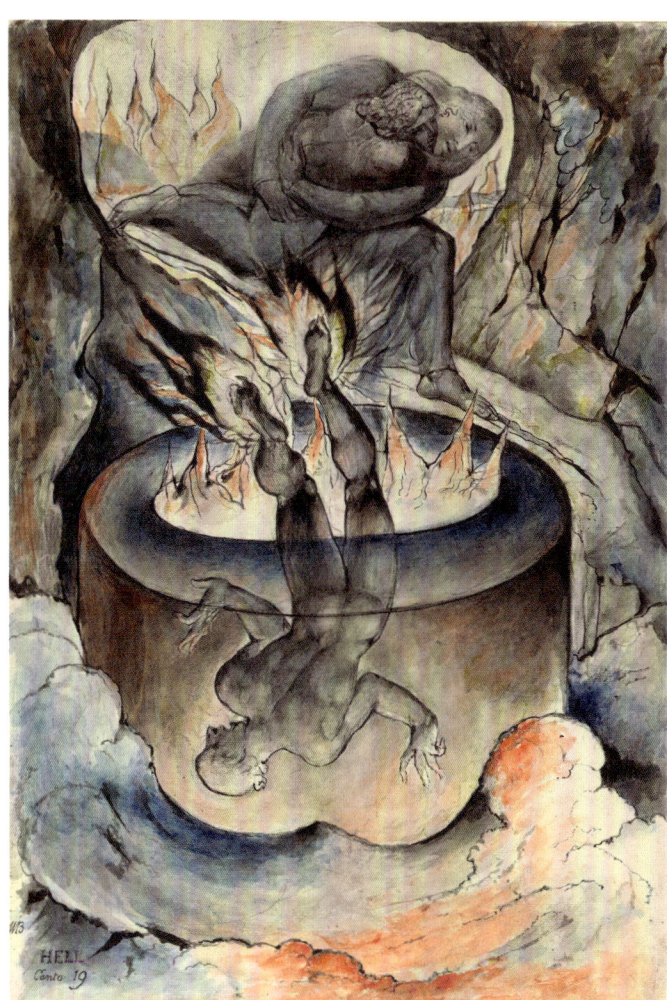

The Simoniac Pope 1824–7
Ink and watercolour
on paper
52.7 × 36.8

The Ascent of the Mountain
of Purgatory 1824–7
Graphite, ink and
watercolour on paper
52.8 × 37.2

OVERLEAF
Mirth and The Youthful Poet's
Dream c.1816–20
Illustrations for Milton's
L'Allegro
Watercolour over graphite
on paper
Each 16.1 × 12.1

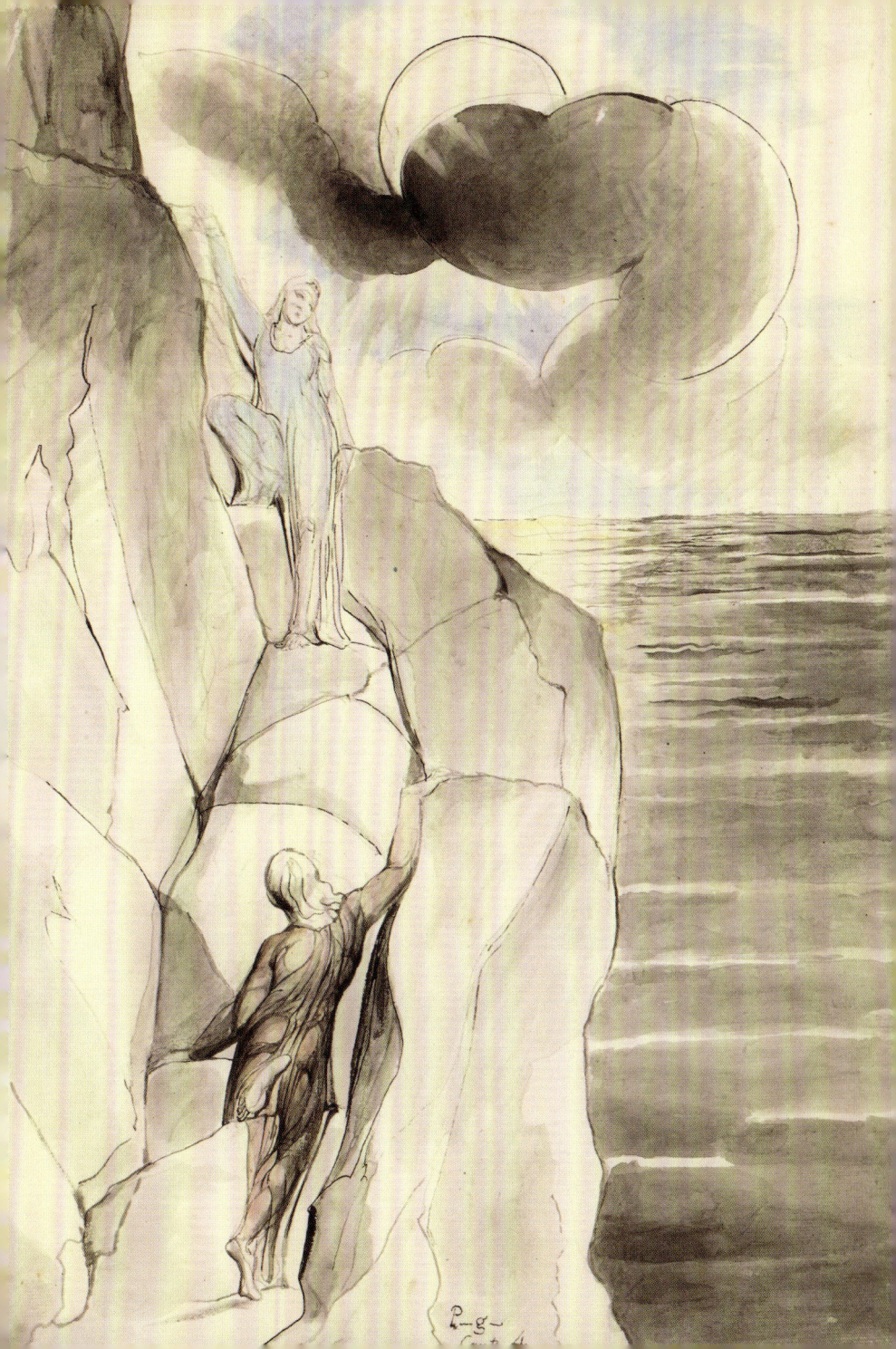

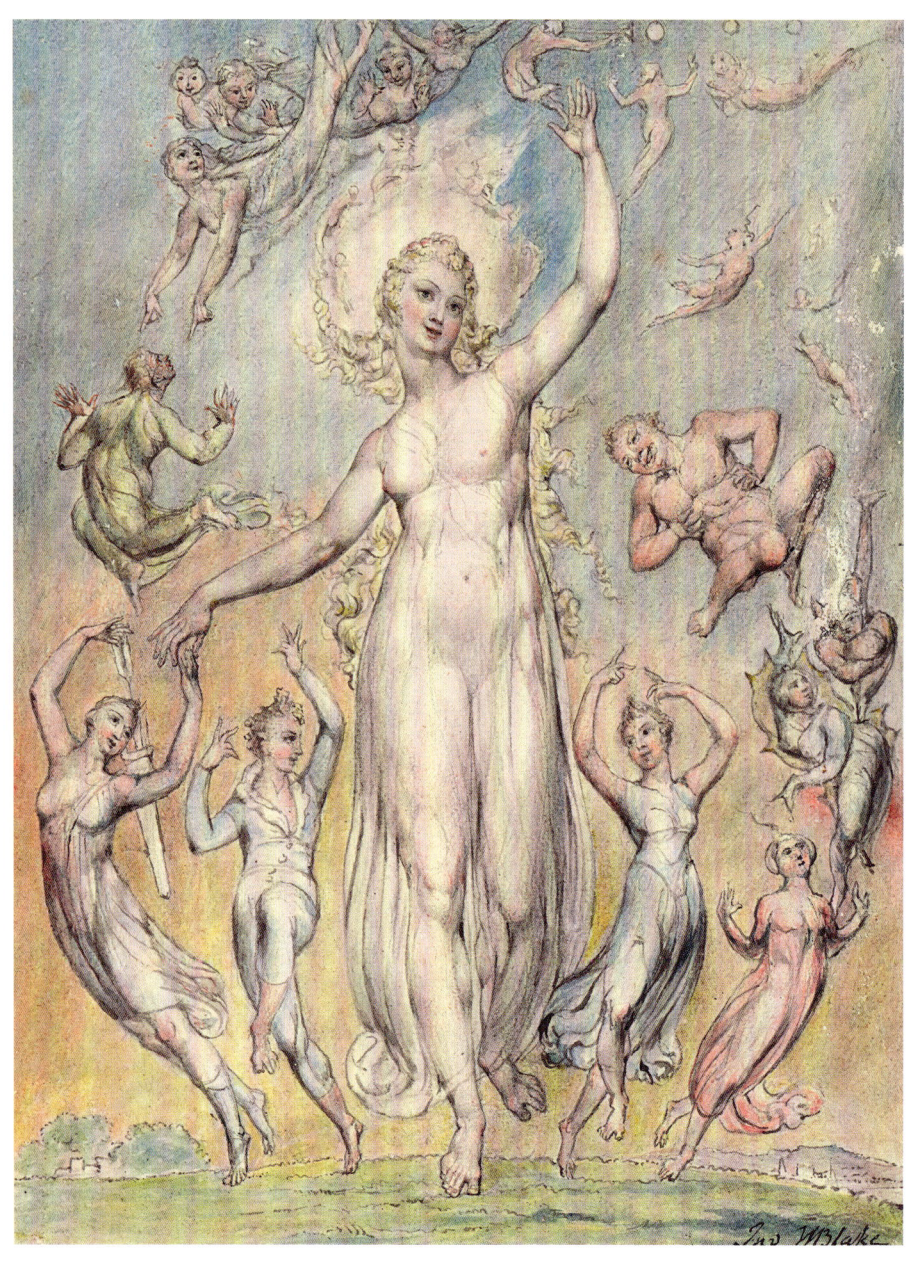

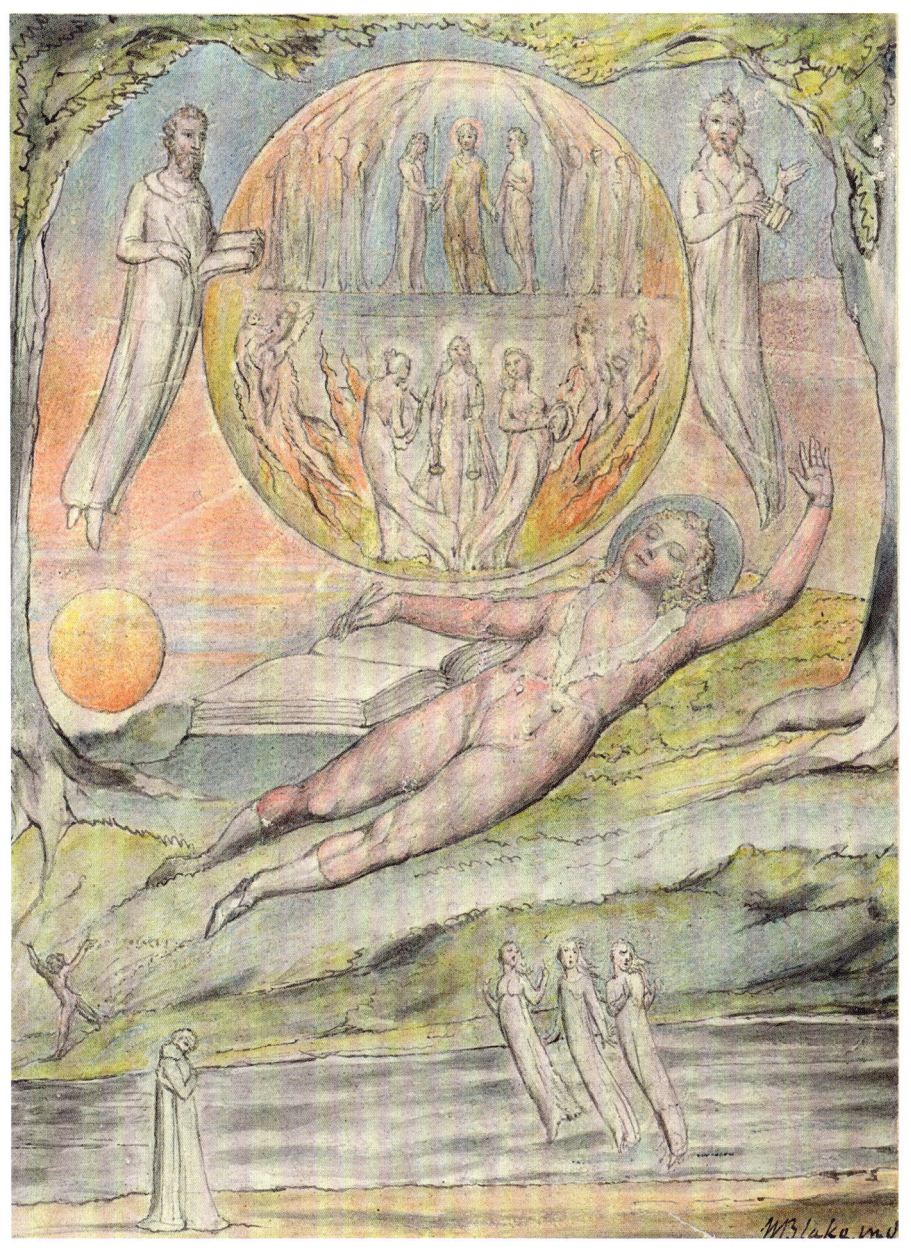

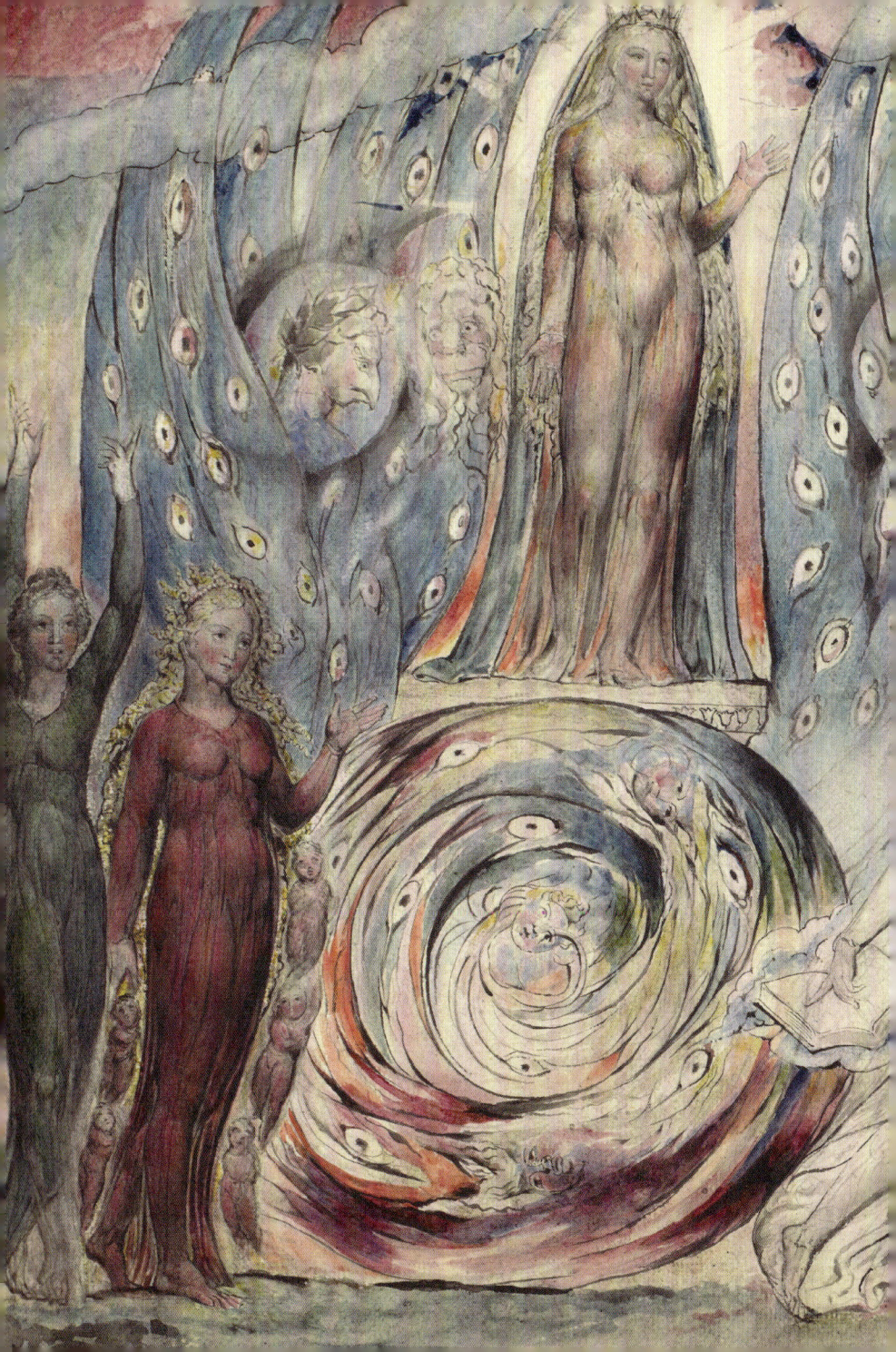

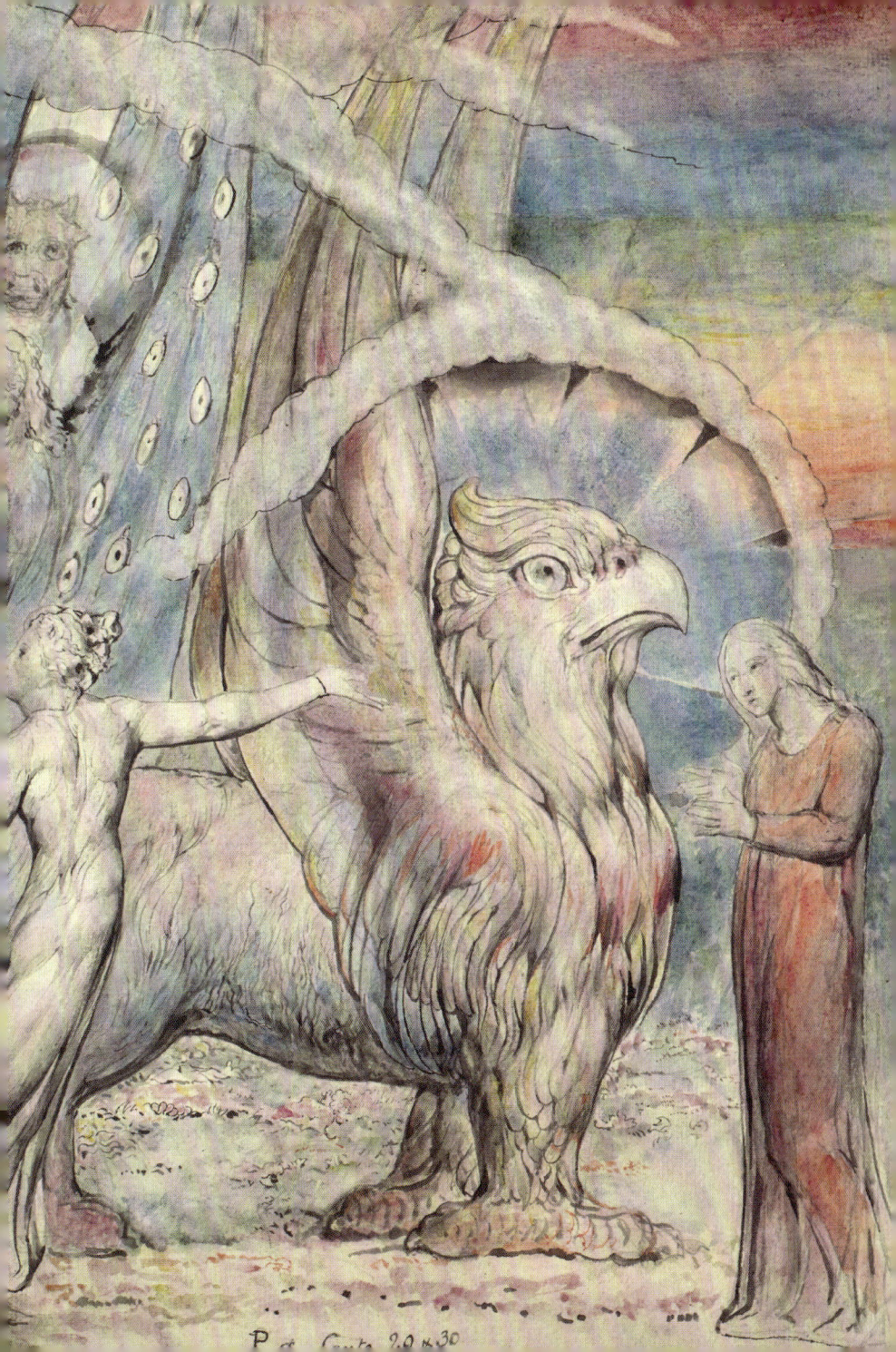

P d Canto 29 & 30

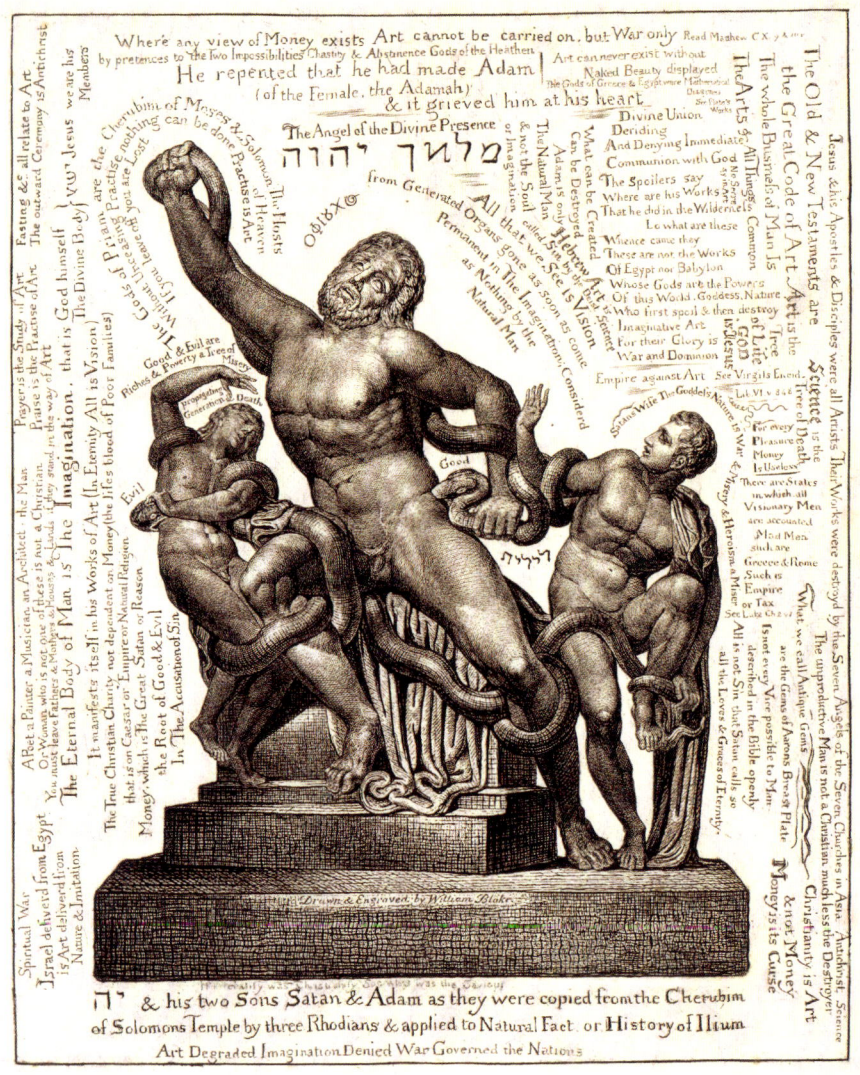

Laocoön 1818
Engraving on paper
27.4 × 22.7

PREVIOUS PAGES
*Beatrice Addressing Dante from
the Car* 1824–7
Ink and watercolour
on paper
37.2 × 52.7

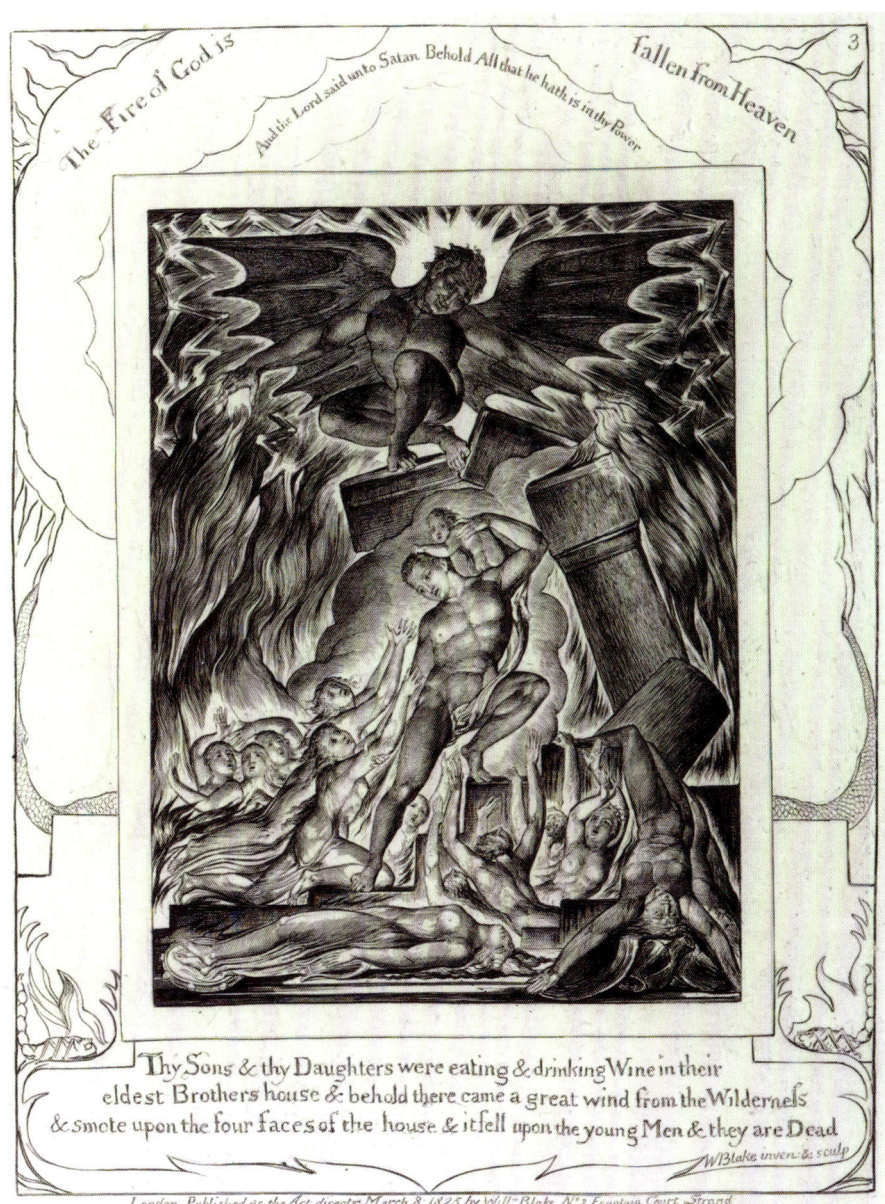

The Fire of God is

And the Lord said unto Satan Behold All that he hath is in thy Power

fallen from Heaven

3

Thy Sons & thy Daughters were eating & drinking Wine in their
eldest Brothers house & behold there came a great wind from the Wilderness
& smote upon the four faces of the house & it fell upon the young Men & they are Dead

WBlake invenit & sculp

London, Published as the Act directs March 8. 1825 by Willm Blake N.º 3 Fountain Court Strand

Job's Sons and Daughters
Overwhelmed by Satan 1825,
reprinted 1874
Engraving on paper
19.7 × 15.3

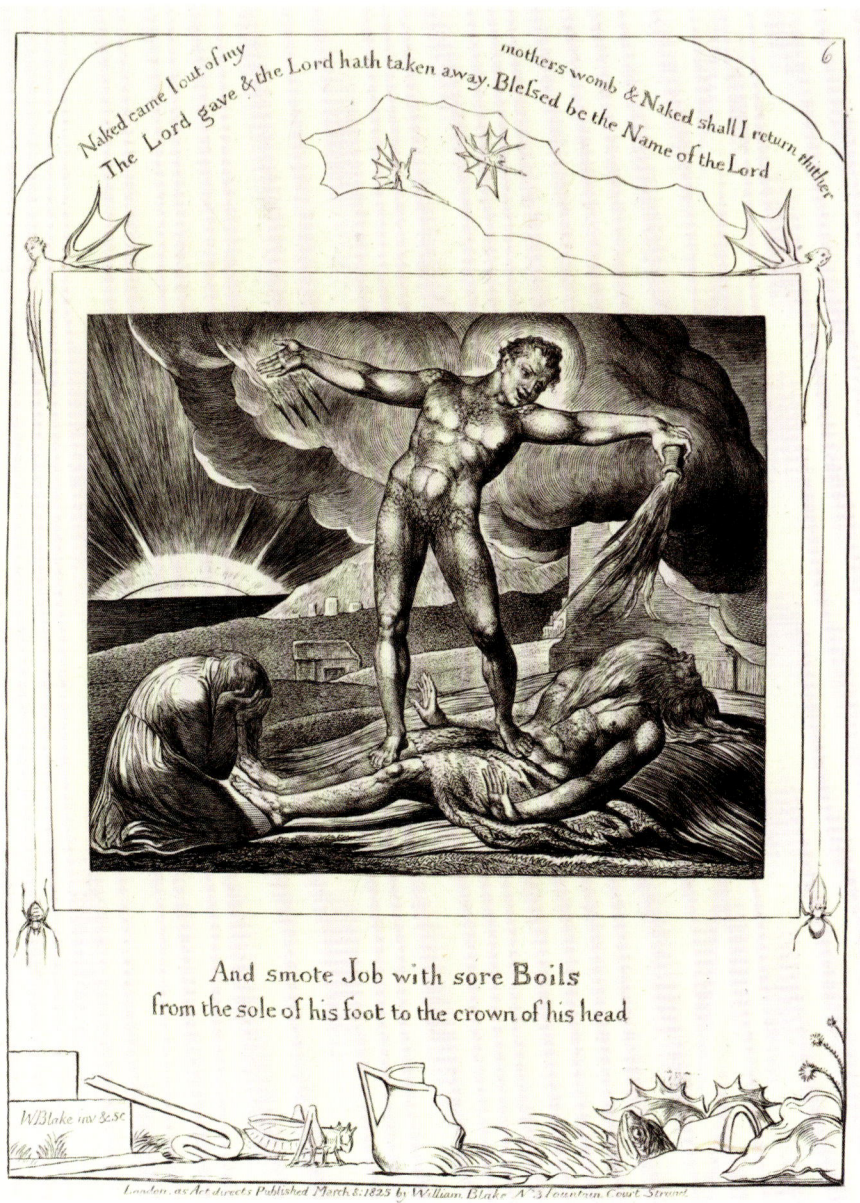

*Satan Smiting Job with Sore
Boils* 1825, reprinted 1874
Engraving on paper
19.8 × 15.3

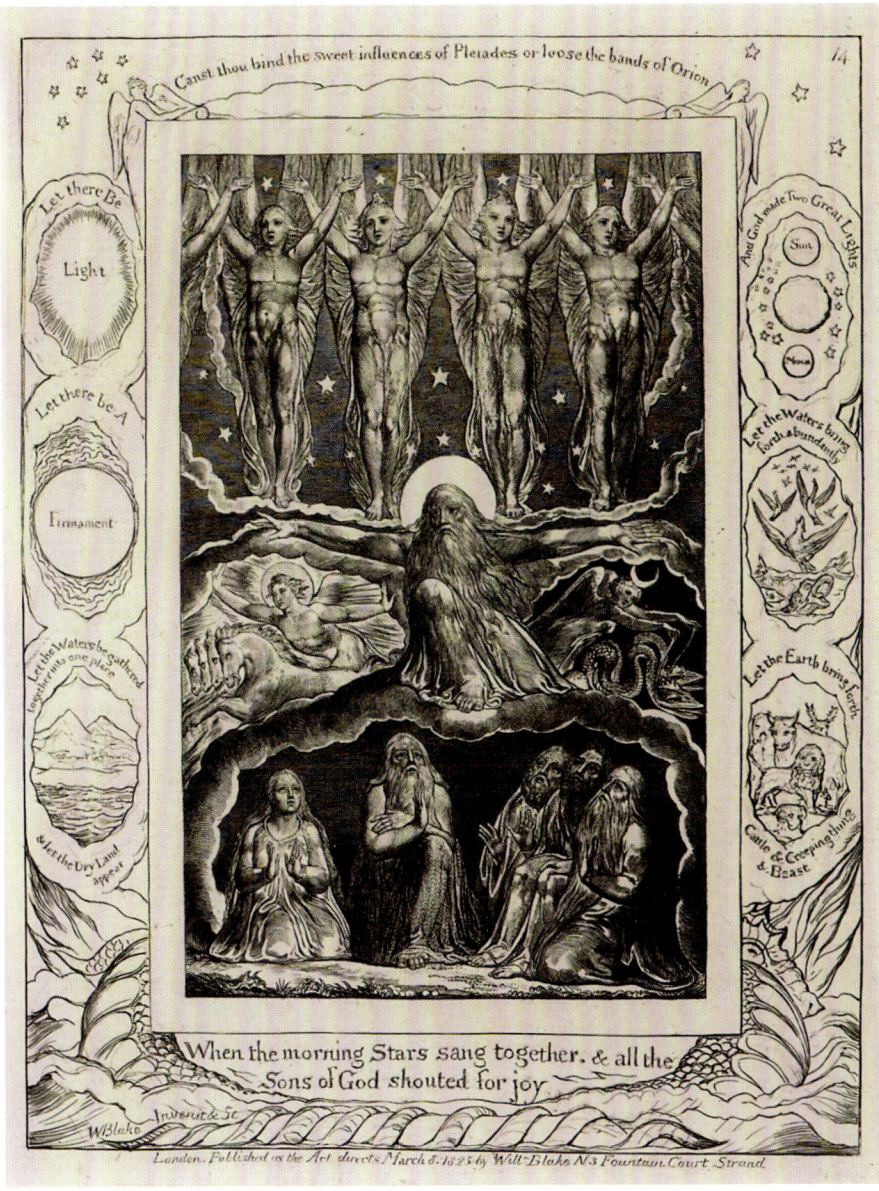

*When the Morning Stars Sang
Together* 1825, reprinted 1874
Engraving on paper
19.1 × 15

NOTES

1. William Blake, *The Marriage of Heaven and Hell*, pl.10.

2. William Blake, *A Descriptive Catalogue of Pictures*, London 1809, p.36 (accessible via the Blake Archive here: https://blakearchive. org/copy/bb32.d?des-cId=bb32.d.te.01). The quotation also appears in David V. Erdman, *The Complete Poetry and Prose of William Blake*, revised edn, Berkeley, CA 1982, p.541.

3. William Blake, letter to Thomas Butts, 10 Jan. 1803.

4. Anne and Alexander Gilchrist, *Life of Blake*, 2nd edn, Cambridge 1880, vol.1, p.243.

5. William Blake, *Satiric Verses and Epigrams*, in Erdman 1982, p.510.

6. Gilchrist and Gilchrist 1880, p.7.

7. William Blake, Annotations to *The Works of Sir Joshua Reynolds*, p.32. In Erdman 1982, p.645.

8. William Blake, 'Public Address', p.11. In Erdman 1982, p.571.

9. Blake 1809, p.1.

10. See Martin Myrone, 'View of William Blake as a Student of the Royal Academi: A Prosopographical Perspective', *Blake/An Illustrated Quarterly*, vol.51, no.2, 2017, paragraph 4, https://blakequarterly.org/ index.php/blake/article/ view/myrone512/pdf, accessed 9 July 2024.

11. William Blake, Annotations to *The Works of Sir Joshua Reynolds*, London 1798, title verso.

12. William Blake, letter to Thomas Butts, 10 Jan. 1803.

13. Gilchrist and Gilchrist 1880, p.410.

14. See Angus Whitehead, '"an excellent saleswoman": The Last Years of Catherine Blake', *Blake/An Illustrated Quarterly*, vol.45, no.3, Winter 2011–12, pp.76–90.

15. Blake, 'The Tyger' (1794), in *The Songs of Experience*, London 1794.

16. William Blake, *Jerusalem*, London 1804/1820, pl.34 [38].

17. William Blake, letter to George Cumberland, postmarked 1 Sept. 1800. More information on the dating of this letter can be found here: https://bq. blakearchive.org/32.1. essick.

18. William Blake, letter to William Hayley, 26 Nov. 1800.

19. William Blake, letter to Thomas Butts, 10 Jan. 1803.

20. See Mark Crosby, '"A Fabricated Perjury": The [Mis]Trial of William Blake', *Huntington Library Quarterly*, vol.72, no.1, 2009, pp.29–37 [34].

21. William Blake, letter to Thomas Butts, 25 April 1803.

22. William Blake, letter to Thomas Butts, 6 July 1803.

23. William Blake, advertisement of *Descriptive Catalogue* (1809). In Erdman 1982, p.528.

24. Blake 1809, p.5.

25. Robert Hunt, *The Examiner*, 17 Sept. 1809; G.E. Bentley, *Blake Records*, New Haven and London 2004, p.283.

26. Blake 1804/1820, plate 34 [38].

27. Robert Essick, quoted in Whitehead 2011–12, paragraph 12.

28. William Blake, letter to John Linnell, 19 May 1826; letter to George Cumberland, 12 April 1827.

29. Bentley 2004, pp.400–1.

30. Louise Wilson, 'To see a world in a grain of sand: a closer look at the "Melbourne Blakes"', National Gallery of Victoria, 16 April 2014, https://www.ngv. vic.gov.au/essay/to-see-a-world-in-a-grain-of-sand-a-closer-look-at-the-melbourne-blakes, accessed 4 July 2024.

31. Blake 1804/1820, plate 77.

FURTHER READING

Peter Ackroyd, *Blake: A Biography*, London 1995.

David V. Erdman, *The Complete Poetry and Prose of William Blake*, revised edn, Berkeley, CA 1982.

John Higgs, *William Blake Now: Why He Matters More Than Ever*, London 2019.

Saree Makdisi, *William Blake and the Impossible History of the 1790s*, Chicago 2003.

Martin Myrone and Amy Concannon, *William Blake*, London 2019.

Jason Whittaker, *Divine Images: The Life and Work of William Blake*, London 2021.

William Blake: Apprentice & Master, exh. cat., Ashmolean Museum, Oxford 2014.

INDEX

Page references in italics indicate images.

CREDITS

First published 2024 by order of the Tate Trustees
by Tate Publishing, a division of Tate Enterprises Ltd,
Millbank, London SW1P 4RG
www.tate.org.uk/publishing

A catalogue record for this book is available from
the British Library

ISBN 978 1 84976 949 5

Distributed in the United States and Canada by
ABRAMS, New York

Library of Congress Control Number applied for

Commissioning Editor: Emma Poulter
Editorial Assistant: Aki Gurung
Production: Juliette Dupire
Picture Researcher: Emma O'Neill
Design: Astrid Stavro Studio
Colour reproduction by DL Imaging, London
Printed and bound in **Italy by Printer Trento S.r.l**

Cover: *Dante Running from the Three Beasts* 1824–7
(detail, see pp.76–7)
Frontispiece: '*Jerusalem*' plate 1 composed c.1804–
20, printed c.1821 (detail, see p.65)

Measurements of artworks are given in
centimetres, height before width and depth

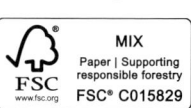

THE AUTHOR
Caroline Anjali Ritchie is a research fellow at
Exeter College, University of Oxford. She is
also author of the book *William Blake and the
Cartographic Imagination*, to be published by
Palgrave Macmillan, London, in 2025.